TRANSLATING THE CURRICULUM

TRANSLATING THE CURRICULUM

*Multiculturalism into
Cultural Studies*

SUSAN HUDDLESTON EDGERTON

ROUTLEDGE

New York • London

Published in 1996 by

Routledge
29 West 35 Street
New York, NY 10001

Published in Great Britain by

Routledge
11 New Fetter Lane
London EC4P 4EE

Library of Congress Cataloging-in-Publication Data

Edgerton, Susan Huddleston, 1955–
    Translating the curriculum : multiculturalism into cultural
studies / Susan Huddleston Edgerton.
      p.   cm.
    Includes bibliographical references and index.
    ISBN 0-415-91400-0. — ISBN 0-415-91401-9 (pbk.)
    1. Multicultural education—United States.   2. Multicultural
education—United States—Curricula.   3. Educational anthropology—
United States.   I. Title.
LC1099.3.E34   1996
370.19'6—dc20
                                         96-7555
                                         CIP

To my parents
Mary Elizabeth Eldridge Huddleston
and
Clifton Monroe Huddleston

Contents

Acknowledgments

WHILE WORKING ON THIS BOOK last July fourth I wrote, "Are those fire-
works I hear just for me? The isolation of a writing life distorts by
putting one either right at the center of the world or spinning eternally
on the periphery. Brilliance or idiocy! The vacillation doesn't linger in
between during the writing days; it is either/or. It is so lonely! And
when it doesn't go well it is also so easy to sink low." But lonely writing
is at its best for me when it provokes a sense of aching desire, a sweet
yearning for distant ones that gives life to the writing of letters. There
were many distant ones, sometimes remembered, sometimes pushed
back, fuelling this work. The writing act *requires* a kind of forgetting
along with remembering. Now that I am here alone in my apartment,
with this final task before me (writing the acknowledgments), I am
forced to remember; and it sometimes hurts to recall how, and how
much, I have learned to forget. So begins the task . . .

This work began as a dissertation a few years ago, so my first remembering goes back to that time. Living in a "graduate student ghetto"
with a number of my peers and friends, our mutual poverty and passion
made for a rare community. That community nurtured me through an
insane summer of rushing to finish before I had to move to Chicago.
Thanks go to YongHwan Lee, David Thomson, Ron Manning, Wen

Song Hwu, and Greg Nixon for urging me on, bringing me food and good company. Greg read every word as it came off the printer, copyedited and critiqued in a manner that made the work better without undermining my already strained confidence.

Mary Ann Doyle, a woman of huge heart, soul and intellect, was, and still is, always available to me, always a multidimensional inspiration. Mary Ann was indispensable during the final moments of completing the bureaucratic tasks that bind dissertations into a final package. She also added her helpful commentary to a more recent version.

John and Layne St. Julien provided loving encouragement and discussion, and have continued to do so as we've made our parallel journeys from Louisiana to Illinois.

For the sharing and comradery of that initial writing, I also want to thank Patrick Slattery, John Konopak, Mary Duchein, Nicole Perraton-Aveles, Angela Lydon, Jeanne Robertson, and Connie Nobles.

Though I have mentioned some of my mentors in the preface, I want to give additional thanks to two here. Cameron McCarthy has offered, and continues to offer, his unflagging friendship and support for my work. My writing and thinking are deeply indebted to his influence. Bill Pinar provided a phenomenal experience for his graduate students at LSU, of whom I was lucky enough to be among. This work is an expression of that relationship, and of a friendship that endures.

A special thanks goes to Peter Taubman, who began reading the dissertation even before it was completed and offered words to help me through. Peter also read a later version, providing an insightful critique.

Thanks to Madeleine Grumet for reading an earlier draft and offering encouragement and comment.

Special thanks also to Mark Perry for reading the second-to-last-version and writing pages of invaluable commentary and suggestion. Mark was generous beyond imagining with his time.

Thanks to Diane Brunner who read and wrote comments to an earlier version. Her work has been an inspiration here as well as in my teaching.

For intellectual and emotional support, I especially want to thank my Chicago friends, Eleanor Binstock, Susie Zeiser, and Ed Berggren. Also, thanks to Ina Pinkney for love and nourishment. (If you don't believe in the food-effects portrayed in *Like Water for Chocolate*, I suggest you visit Ina's Kitchen here in Chicago!)

A very special thanks to my friend and colleague Bill Ayers for reading my work whenever I asked him to, and commenting regardless of how busy he was.

Other colleagues at the University of Illinois are in here too: Bill Schubert, Vicki Chou, Steve Tozer, Annette Henry, Michelle Parker, Joe Becker, Artin Goncu, Caroline Heller, Eileen Ball, Terri Thorkildsen, the late John Nicholls, David Hansen, Marilyn Geron, Hal Adams, and Chris Pappas. And I thank my dean, Larry Braskamp, for allowing me to take a leave of absence in which to write this and do other related work.

Thanks also to Bernardine Dohrn for her friendship and commentary.

Others who have provided friendship and intellectual and emotional nourishing from a distance are Janet Miller, Florence Krall, Mary Aswell Doll, and my good friend of twenty-five years, Larry Waldron.

In Chicago, Sylvia Babbin helped me find courage and a better connection to children and elders.

Thanks to the women who participated in a written dialogue with Susie Zeiser and myself—a dialogue essential to the completion of this book: Mary Doll, Maxine Greene, Liz Ellsworth, Janet Miller, Mimi Orner, and Susie's friends, Bernardine, Rachel, and Ann.

Thanks are due for their continual encouragement to Warren Crichlow, Glen Hudak, Deborah Britzman, Alice Pitt, Jo Ann Pagano, Bill Stanley, Ted Aoki, Jim Hall, and Alan Carey Webb.

Special thanks to my loving family, Mary Beth and Cliff Huddleston, Amy Redding, and Pat Stetson.

I feel so very fortunate to have had Jayne Fargnoli as editor of my first book. Her talent shines in her abilities to simultaneously encourage, critique, and to press one on without hammering.

Finally, thanks are due in more ways and on more levels than I can possibly mention here to Michael Ruggles. His loving support in these final days of writing has been indispensable.

Preface

THE PROMISE

On "Autobiography," an "Autobiography"

MUCH OF WHAT I WRITE ABOUT is not joyful. The same must be said about what I teach. It's not joyful because the work is so often about histories of trauma and testimonies to those histories. The traumas range from grand-scale genocide to more individual levels, though these levels are inextricably related. Mark C. Taylor writes:

> The history of society and culture is, in large measure, a history of the struggle with the endlessly complex problems of difference and otherness. . . . Is difference tolerable? . . . The ghettos of Europe, America, and South Africa, the walls in Germany [now "gone"], China, and Korea, and battlefields throughout the world testify to the urgency of the issue of difference. A century that opened with the publication of *The Interpretation of Dreams* should have learned by now that the repressed never goes away but always returns—sometimes violently. As we approach the close of the millennium, the fires ignited in the ovens of Europe threaten to encompass the entire globe. Holocaust is one response to difference. (1987, xxi)

So what does it mean when I leave a class, or a writing session, feeling elated by its seeming success, by a sense of having accomplished something, when that "success" or "something" involves mutual recognition of such dire subject matter? Such a question leads me inescapably back to myself, assuming my "self" is more accessible to me than another self in terms of psychic functioning, of motivation and desire. Autobiographical writing, despite claims of its impossibility, its contrivance, its deceptions, is a necessary part of the work presented here as well as in my classroom. As a consequence I have worked hard to insert myself, or at least not to hide myself, in the pages that follow. I may not have always succeeded.

At the same time, in my teaching and writing, I want to encourage other responses to difference than degrees of violence. Excavating repressed histories of violence, however, is a necessary first step. It is only when we take a good, hard look at what comes out, that we can begin the talk and work of joy—joy produced by the positive potentialities and effects of difference, by the learning that can (but does not always) come from collective and individual suffering, by the life-affirmation of honesty and commitment to democratic and loving transformation.

This work is ambitious, perhaps to a fault. Such is probably the nature of something called "cultural studies" in its efforts to embrace, attack, employ and deploy many disciplines at once. But such an approach is my destiny, it seems, as it characterizes the very manner in which I came to the study of education and curriculum.

Both parents were educators: my father a professor of special education and a "Skinnerian" in the latter part of that career, and my mother an occupational therapist at a local "special school" for many years. From my father's bookshelf I pulled A.S. Neill's *Summerhill* at the age of 14 or 15, and therefrom ensued a flood of rage directed at my schooling, high school officials, and often my father as well. Reading also began to include some literary works—especially "historical fiction." In particular, and as described more fully later, I engaged with works of romantic historical fiction by Gwin Bristow about antebellum Louisiana, and Hawthorne's *The Scarlet Letter*. These works were the real teachers, or so I felt at the time—uncharitable as that probably was to some of my school teachers.

At the same time, and well before, I was an avid watcher of nature in the neighborhood woods. While I did not know the names of all the regional flora and fauna, I at least recognized most of them, and knew what I could eat, touch, or otherwise use, what specific smells were, and what could harm me. Reading, early on, was largely about nature and "science." Fascinated in particular by smell, I forgot for a while about my earlier resolve to rescue other children from the schooling I had, and so pursued a career in organic chemistry as far as a year toward a doctorate in "natural products synthesis." But the urge toward teaching and learning across many disciplines prevailed (I was nowhere near ready to be a "good chemist"). Eventually, it brought me to a high school teaching assignment, where I taught all sciences offered, in addition to a course in cultural anthropology, for four years.

Being a teacher felt so right. But still I didn't know enough. (I've since come to realize that one never does . . . unless one finally relinquishes the consumer-fanatic approach to knowing and yields to the flow of the interminable process.) Seeking to extend my knowledge then, however, positioned me to meet William Pinar, who encouraged me to take up graduate studies in curriculum at Louisiana State University. There I met Cameron McCarthy, who introduced me to cultural studies, and who continues to inspire me in that direction today. I also pursued studies in literature and literary criticism with Richard Moreland of the English department at the same time that I was learning about the linkages among literature, curriculum, and life in my own department from Bill Pinar, Jacques Daignault, and Tony Whitson. Leslie Roman connected it all to feminist studies. William Doll and Ron Good helped me to link all of that to my ongoing interest in science, cognition and natural history. With so many disciplines tugging my sleeves at a given moment, an attraction to what is called cultural studies, primarily through what was the British Cultural Studies movement, makes much sense. But I offer this preface with a promise to elaborate that connection and rationale later. Many have already worked to define and describe this style of cultural studies, so that part of this work will stand on prior pieces to a great extent. For now, I simply want to offer a slice of my progression as preface to the work that follows.

A few astute readers and critics of some of my earlier writing observed to me that I had written nothing of the "how" when I reported events—perhaps I may call them 'educative events'—in my teacher education classrooms, whereby some students were moved to write what must have been personally difficult pieces about transformations out of ignorance of various orders. Of course, such events do not happen all the time or for everyone in my classes. But a good part of my writing is about when transformation seems to occur in connection to classroom experiences, and I could not deny to my critics that I had not really articulated, in any coherent manner, how it happened when it did. These critics were not to be put off or dismissed—they were members of my dissertation committee. Later, the critics were students in my teacher education courses.

Since those earliest times, I have thought more about the 'how' of such teaching/learning situations. This 'how' is still not easy or simple, but it certainly bears elaboration. I think the best responses to "how?" are found somewhere in the ideas termed "somatic translation" (Robinson 1991), "somatic knowledge" (Heshusius 1994) and "bodyreading" (Grumet 1988a). The responses are about intelligence and reason that defies most attempts at a mind/body split. This automatically rules out the possibility of "measurement." I try to write responses to the 'how' question here, the questions of practice and "the practical," without use of the inherently impossible crutch of most of what passes for methodology in scholarly work in the social sciences. To write about that in the manner promised, however, requires a great deal of support through writing about other than that, and maybe beyond that. There are histories (stories) to be remembered and told; there are lines of inquiry to be followed and traced; there are people, objects and events to be acknowledged; there are mysteries to be unsuccessfully plumbed (as they may be part of The Mystery).

These are the last lines in a novel I'll never forget (I'll forget neither lines nor novel):

> Make me, remake me. You are free to do it and I am free to let you because look, look. Look where your hands are. Now. (Morrison 1992, 229)

Such is the nature of text; and in some ways all of our attempts to address one another are textual and linguistic, including body-reading and body-languages. To begin a book that is at the same time theoretical, autobiographical, indebted to something called "cultural studies" (which is to say "antidisciplinary studies"), and dedicated to love and democracy, and is also a book about literature and teaching could be paralyzing to me without Toni Morrison's reminder. She reminds me that though I have thought a lot about memory, reading, writing, loving, justice, teaching, and learning, the way my representations of those thoughts are taken up is beyond my control. Nonetheless, that "I am free to let you" imparts a particular responsibility to me—one that I don't take lightly. In the same manner, teaching is a process that imparts a responsibility, and is one that I try never to take too lightly (or too heavily).

Susan Huddleston Edgerton
Chicago, Illinois

1

Introduction

It is written in rage and love, without which there is no hope.
> —Paulo Freire, *Pedagogy of Hope*

We might then model to our children how we can live in this society without succumbing to it, without giving up our dreams and aspirations for education. Teachers can become witnesses to the notion that intelligence and learning can lead to other worlds, not just the successful exploitation of this one.
> —William Pinar, "Dreamt into Existence by Others"

As a high school teacher in 1987, I recall that crystallized moment standing over the copy machine, a central meeting place, with several articles from popular news magazines and newspapers about two new bestsellers in hardback. Those books were E. D. Hirsch's *Cultural Literacy* and Allan Bloom's *The Closing of the American Mind*. The articles initially caught my attention because I was teaching a cultural anthropology class in which we were focussing on "contemporary American culture." I was struck by the odd coincidence of these books and the media hype accompanying them. What was going on? These books were receiving far more attention than any other books by academics that I could recall. Bestsellers in hardback were usually relegated to "pulp fiction," gossipy biographies, or self-help books.

Since that time, I have been a closer follower of the debates—both in popular media and in academia—about culture. The complexity of these debates, and especially the confusion within, among, and between academic and more public discourses, is difficult to miss. Another reason for my intellectual affinity to thinking through a "field" called *cultural studies* is that I sense that a cultural studies approach is a good way to come to grips with some of the confusion . . . a better way, in fact, than most of the theoretical and practical work that falls under the sign of *multiculturalism* or *multicultural education*. So "what IS cultural studies, anyway?" (Johnson 1983, emphasis added). Writing about that in sufficient detail, and how it links to the larger project of this book, will take time and space in the next chapter and beyond. Suffice it to say for now that cultural studies involves translations across both academic and nonacademic discourses and across academic disciplines. The term *translation* is self-consciously and carefully selected for nuances that take it beyond simple *communication*, into a more intimate, ambiguous, and in some senses tentative realm. This, too, will be taken up in more detail as the page numbers grow. Good translation is also linked to good teaching. Cultural studies requires interdisciplinary translations because it is *antidisciplinary*. That is, it attempts to question at every turn the ways disciplinary boundaries are drawn. What kind of work is being done, and what effects are produced, when a department of literature seeks to distinguish and distance itself from a department of curriculum, for example, and vice versa? (Such a question is not unrelated to issues around cultural diversity. That is, what effects are produced when one group seeks to distinguish and distance itself from another?)

Teacher educators have been challenged recently to do a better job at bringing the discourses of cultural studies into the field. At the same time, scholars of cultural studies (in fields such as literature, film, media, and communications) are criticized for disregarding education as a field (Giroux 1992, 1994). Why, Henry Giroux wonders, have "so few academics . . . incorporated cultural studies into the language of educational reform" (1994, 278) when cultural studies as a field is "about the hottest thing in humanities and social-science research right now" (*Chronicle of Higher Education*, 1993; cited in Giroux, 1994)? This book represents my own attempt to do a piece of that work. My sense is that there exist problems with translation between disciplinary boundaries and academic departments that will require a mixing of discourses and a more aggressive effort to speak across those boundaries in our classrooms, at our common meetings, and in our writing. As an example of a place within academia where mixing might have occurred (but didn't), I recall reading a paper that was presented at the 1993 meeting of the Midwest Modern Language Association by a well-known literary critic that insisted the new trend in research for the language fields is toward pedagogy. Later at that same conference, after a keynote address by another well-known literary critic, someone in the audience felt compelled to rise and bemoan the "use" of literature within the social sciences. I confess that I remained silent, overwhelmed by the irony. Part of my effort here is to redress my own silence.

Like Giroux (1994), my work is addressed to my colleagues in education as well as to those in other departments who seem to be taking the "turn to pedagogy" that some suggest is timely and necessary. It pleases me to see so much work directed at the classroom coming from outside the field of education. That might signify that, at long last, education as a discipline for thought, study and reflection is gaining the legitimacy it has needed and deserved but not received. However, it disturbs me to note that most of the work coming from fields in modern languages, communications, and philosophy about pedagogy (see, e.g., Felman 1987, 1992; Morton and Zavarzadeh 1991; Nelson 1986; Spivak 1993; hooks 1994; Gallop 1995[1]) mention few, if any, of the works of my colleagues in education who have been struggling with similar pedagogical questions for twenty years or more. (Not to mention education and curriculum theorists who wrote in the first quarter of this century about similar problematics, such as John Dewey, Harold Rugg, Hilda Taba, W.E.B. DuBois, and Carter G. Woodson). When education academics are mentioned in works about pedagogy that identify with cultural studies, or aspects of cultural studies, they are almost always the same few: Paulo Freire, Henry Giroux, Michael Apple, and/or Peter McLaren. Indeed, Freire is often referred to as though he is a new discovery despite the fact he has been publishing for decades. And while it is satisfying to see that even these few colleagues are being widely read, especially as they have produced much fine work, the field is much larger than this. It is composed of many other intelligent women and men—almost never mentioned in such works— who have important insights into pedagogies concerned with culture and cultural studies (see, e.g., authors in the edited collection by McCarthy and Crichlow, *Race, Representation, Identity in Education,* 1993). My point, directed at noneducationist pedagogical writers, is that four men (Freire, Giroux, Apple, and McLaren) do not adequately represent all of us in the teaching fields who have cultural studies concerns and works. I'm not suggesting that males (especially, it might be implied, white males such as Giroux, Apple, and McLaren) cannot write well about cultural studies in education—only that cultural studies in education needs a more diverse representation in order not to betray many of its own agendas, even as it still very much needs those men. Further, it is important that I note that I do read many of those who write about pedagogy but who are not housed in colleges of education (e.g., Felman 1992; Gallop 1995; Graff 1992, 1993; hooks 1995; Griffin 1992); I learn from them, enjoy them, often assign them in my classes, and hence am not suggesting by any means that they be ignored. My plea is simply for greater dialogue and respect. Such is in the best interests of all who are genuinely concerned with the problem of pedagogy and committed to the survival of public education, because the public perception of the fields in education *does* matter to those projects.

Given all of this, I offer one narrative about cultural studies and its implications for pedagogies—especially pedagogies that go by the name *multicultural education.* This is addressed to both my colleagues in education who might be curious as to what some of us mean when we invoke the name *cultural studies,* and to cultural studies scholars in other departments who might be curious about how one education academic integrates cultural studies into her work and life.

But my concern and distress lie beyond the discourses of academia over multiculturalism and cultural studies. Poor translations abound among academic, kindergarten through twelfth-grade schooling, and popular media discourses about the meanings of culture, multiculture, and cultural studies, often ending with a clipped dismissal of all to the tyranny of "political correctness," purportedly rife among scholars especially, and in schooling generally. While critical academics are necessarily honing technical languages for thinking about subjectivities, deconstruction, marginality, essentialism, and many other such social, political and philosophical lines of inquiry, the rest of the education system worries (perhaps at its best) about self-esteem, attitudes, and "telling the truth" in histories and literatures, where what counts as "truth" is as narrowly conceived as ever, even if the stories offer new characters. In representing such phenomena, the most popular media most often present a confused, disjointed, and angry proliferation of labels and slogans conflated under too-few terms and phrases that emanate from universities and schools. If universities and schools (including colleges of education, where school teachers are certified) do not even understand one another when presumably speaking of the same things (multicultural education, diversity, etc.), then what indeed must the rest of the public perceive as "the problem"? I am under no illusion that this book might be so widely read as to address all of these audiences. However, if I succeed at all in accomplishing my goals, this book might begin such a multilayered conversation somewhere, somehow. It might instigate a "translation without a master" (Rajchmann 1991) between some who do read this book and some who do not.

This work is an *act* of cultural studies as I understand it—especially as it holds ties to British cultural studies. And it is an act of faith and love for a movement, for people, and for a set of texts that began for me much of the work I most want to do. My reading of works with that evasive label surely enabled this work. My project is, in part, to bring what has been called cultural studies to bear upon curriculum, and to do that through the debates around multicultural education, the humanities, and what constitutes "Western culture." *Western culture* is flanked by quotation marks due to my doubts about its clear and locatable existence—especially in the United States. There is a practical reason for my choosing these debates in that it is only through the sometimes forced inculcation of what is called multicultural education that is taking place in this country, that many practitioners and theorists of curriculum are coming into some contact with the problematics of culture and marginality. But far too often what gets called *multicul-*

tural education is weakened and watered-down through appropriation by those who would use it as a new way to silence rage rather than honestly and faithfully address it. Sometimes it is weakened despite the best of intentions, as will be discussed in the next chapter. Although I am obviously critical of much of what has been called multicultural education, I in no way wish to dismiss or diminish in my arguments the many good works that have fallen under that banner. I do, however, wish to provide a rationale for going beyond many of the models and approaches to multicultural education that continue to hold sway in school practices.

The canon debates are critical to this project as well because they are debates about *culture*—its definition as a general term and as a concept in particular contexts. Hence, these debates impact upon decisions around curriculum at all levels of the educational enterprise. Some of the necessary insights for dealing with these problems, I believe, are made possible for students of teacher education through readings of literary works authored by members of marginalized groups (from within the U.S. as well as "Third World" countries, such as many in the Caribbean and Latin America which have explicit historical ties to the U.S. and to the "West" generally), and by drawing these readings into conversation with philosophy, history, social theory, and students themselves via reflective writings about their own school, life, and reading experiences. Such a conversation also fruitfully involves "canonized" literary works viewed from the perspective of encounters between such works and marginalized ones.[2]

Literary works of marginalized groups can provide a passage to a shifting of the discourse away from conceptions of multiculturalism as something we "add on" to the curriculum, "do for" marginalized groups, or as a means to simply "change attitudes." Such a shift away is a shift toward a more fluid and thoughtful "discourse of encounters" in its abrogation of the problem of representation—representation as it concerns such entities and notions as identity, culture, and civilization—and in its problematization of notions of cultural translation.[3] Literary works can serve as a kind of counterscreen in a field of other varieties of texts that often tend to screen (reduce and represent) societies, cultures, and individual experience. Social theory alone does not

6

do it, because most social theory that appears in widely accessible publications is trapped within discursive forms that tend to privilege the language/expressions of white middle-class western academics. These texts talk *about* those often excluded from such discourses, whereas literary texts written by those most excluded *speak* lives as they are, or might be, lived. Language is of the body, and literary language most often honors that inalienable connection.

I support these claims, in part, through demonstrations of such "conversations" involving literary works by Toni Morrison, Ralph Ellison, Jamaica Kincaid, William Faulkner, and others. Particular authors were selected for various reasons, including powerful attachments to, and/or representations of place; writings that engage "canonical" works (or, for example, in the case of Faulkner, *are* canonical works which speak of cross-cultural encounters); and writings that demonstrate the power of cross-cultural encounters and imagination (Harris 1989). Some student and personal autobiographical work will also be included in these demonstrations.

I defend my choice to limit my discussions of multicultural education and cultural studies primarily to issues of race and gender, with emphasis on relations between black and white, by virtue of such issues being especially pressing in the particular time and place in which I have conducted my studies—in the deep South, Louisiana, and in the deeply segregated "northern South," Chicago, Illinois. Also, I contend that much of the theorizing that comes from this study is translatable to issues around difference and domination more generally, though applications must be attentive to local contexts. Encounters, both historical and contemporary, that occur in specific *places* are also significant to these approaches to literature and theory (Pinar 1991). Autobiography provides a conjuncture with literature for exploring local context.

I do my work here through a primary focus on philosophical problems that underpin intertextual readings of certain works of contemporary literature and the attendant literary criticism, and on autobiography as both a theoretical and practical problem in my teacher education classrooms. The autobiographical works included are themselves much inspired by literature and philosophy. Discovering the connections, cross-cultural and cross-temporal, among literary works and readers' lives, makes possible the work of *translation without a master*—that is, translation that does not impose the usual extra burdens of translation onto those with least power. The study and use of literature here is aimed at building webs of differences, highlighting overarching commonalities or nodes of intersection, so that languages can become embodied. In this way languages might now be translated, creating historical and cross-cultural imagination, literacy of the imagination, empathy, hope, and faith.

A Map of this Study

The second chapter takes an extremely brief excursion into recent history and critique of multicultural education, offering a slightly less brief history of cultural studies, followed by a framing of some public debates around multiculturalism and the humanities, in the hope of setting a context from which my work has emerged. My project is intended, in part, to address the problem of an undertheorized and co-opted multicultural education. The overall focus of my efforts is to expose the workings of an alternative to "illiteracy of the imagination" (Harris 1989). It is hoped that such an exposure can enter the debates around multiculturalism as a challenge to the narrow vision of mainstream, dominant discourse, as well as to some of those views opposing the mainstream. It challenges those who continue to use a language of simple or binary opposition exclusively, thereby allowing that which is opposed to set the terms of the debate.

The shifting and sifting problematics of identity, difference, culture, and politics that underpin any classroom in contemporary American schools provoke theoretical/philosophical thinking. For me such thinking came to themes of marginality, essentialism, translation, and love. Each of those themes drew me inexorably into the other in chapter three. *Marginality* is viewed as a complex and dynamic interaction among social and individual subjectivities. It is insufficient to view it in simple opposition to centrality or dominance. *Essentialism*—reduction of ideas, phenomena, social actors to positive transcendental essences—

is a problem that emerges out of attempts to discuss oppressions and subjectivities on the basis of race and gender. This problem is approached from feminist and poststructural philosophical perspectives. Given the problematics of marginality and essentialism, communication across difference becomes particularly challenging. The term communication is insufficient as a referent for this problem as it carries connotative baggage from overuse in such areas as popular psychology. To indicate the greater difficulty, complexity, and multidirectionality involved in the construction of an educational space for cross-cultural conversation, I have chosen to explore the notion of *translation*.

Such "communication theorizing," I believe, remains insufficient without consideration of the powerful significance of place (Pinar 1991). Serres's (1982b) notion of "local pockets" of knowledge and communication as well as Deleuze and Guattari's (1983) "group-subjects" will provide some of the theoretical support. Encounters within (translation across difference within) differ from but inform and are informed by encounters between, and are explored through the literary examples in the next chapter as well.

Finally, this translation can not be understood outside notions of *love*. This word has been appropriated (made kitsch) repeatedly such that one is afraid to use the term—especially in theoretic works. I intend to reclaim it. It is about power. If it were not about power, it would not be so often stolen. Love is also about power that is dynamic rather than static and asymmetrical. With Immanuel Levinas I want to suggest throughout that the preoccupation in Western philosophy with ontology (as "first philosophy") is misplaced, and should be replaced with ethics as first.

> This is the question of the meaning of being: not the ontology of the understanding of that extraordinary verb, but the ethics of its justice. The question *par excellence* or the question of philosophy. Not "Why being rather than nothing?", but how being justifies itself. (Levinas 1989, 86, emphasis in original)

That makes this book ultimately about *love*, and it reformulates the curriculum question "What knowledge is of most worth?" to "What knowledges best enable us to care for ourselves, one another, and the nonhuman world?" Or, the question might also be framed as follows: "What knowledges best enable us to minimize violence to ourselves, one another, and the nonhuman world?" Framed in this way, the question implicitly privileges the standpoint of those suffering the greatest violences; of those "carrying the burdens of social inequality" (Connell cited in McCarthy 1993, 301). Curriculum emerging from such a question is a curriculum of rage, love, and hope. It makes possible good translations.

Chapter four consists of readings of literary works that serve as demonstrations of the theoretical problematics framed in chapter three. The readings are generated in such a way as to highlight the translation and subsequent conversation that takes place between and among certain texts. Through the literary, sometimes explicitly autobiographical, examples of both black and white southern American authors, as well as some African-Caribbean authors, I hope to expose the way in which encounters between are constitutive of and are constituted by place. These texts and readings serve as examples for possible inclusions in a teacher education course as they are primary sources for a cultural studies curriculum.

Chapter five deals with the idea of autobiography written in parallel with literary and various theoretical readings in a teacher education course. This chapter discusses autobiography theory and provides an example of my own rereading of, and autobiographical writing with, a work of historical fiction that I initially read as a fourteen-year-old. The novel is set in Louisiana, my childhood home. This provides a passage for a demonstration of the significance of place. I have included a sample of student autobiography produced from a class I taught for preservice teachers in which my ideas for this project were explored.

Finally, chapter six summarizes my position and return to the debates around multiculturalism, cultural studies, and the humanities in order to situate this work among them. From this, the discussion moves to one of implications for the curriculum field with respect to teacher education based in, and working toward, cultural studies curricula.

2

Multiculturalism into Cultural Studies

BACKGROUND AND RATIONALE

The multiculturalist strategy of adding diversity to the dominant school cur-
riculum serves, paradoxically, to legitimate the dominance of Western
culture in educational arrangements in the United States. Multiculturalists
have simply failed to provide a systematic critique of the ideology of
"Westernness" that is ascendant in curriculum and pedagogical practices in
education. Instead, proponents articulate a language of inclusion.
                                        —Cameron McCarthy, "After the Canon"

MULTIPLE MODELS and practices of multicultural education have
by now been multiply defined and critiqued from multiple
political orientations. Many of you reading this will have read accounts
of the recent history of multicultural education in the United States, as
well as criticisms of same. Most compelling for me are the histories and
critiques from those who are sympathetic (i.e., the "Left," or "radical")
to the larger goals of multicultural education (e.g., McCarthy 1988,
1993; Sleeter and Grant 1987; Sleeter 1993; Gay 1987), though occasionally those criticisms intersect with unsympathetic ("Right," or

"conservative") criticisms of multicultural education (e.g., Ravitch 1990; Ravitch and Finn 1987; Cheney 1988, 1989; Bennett 1984, 1988). Now one finds criticisms of various models and approaches to multicultural education, usually of K–12 and teacher multicultural education, scattered throughout the education literature. Some critiques are embedded in texts that call for a different, "critical" multiculturalism (e.g., Kanpol & McLaren 1995). It would be an overwhelming and unnecessary task to attempt to reconstruct this body of work in any detail here. Rather, I'll rapidly reiterate what I consider to be some of the strongest critiques of some of the most commonly repeated versions of multicultural education in order to link that debate to national debates over the humanities (which also touch K–12 schools), and to the more challenging versions of multiculturalism which link it to Cultural Studies.

Cultural deprivation models are among the first to arrive on the scene and the first to be soundly denounced, though that is not to say that versions of "cultural deprivation" do not continue to hold the imaginations of many who teach and many who determine curricula. This model assumes at base that there are identifiable cultures or cultural forms that are originally, and fatally or tragically "deprived" of what is most valuable for a quality life. It is easy to imagine here from whence comes the measure of all those materials and experiences constituting a quality life, and which sort of culture most possesses those materials and embodies those experiences. Yes, it is the "dominant culture," the mythical norm. And, "at this moment in history, that norm is young, White, heterosexual, Christian, able-bodied, thin, middle-class, English-speaking, and male" (Ellsworth 1989, 323).

The much-repeated arguments against such a model are often eventually revisited in various forms to critique other models, those ostensibly *not* about deprivation, but about "harmony" and "changing attitudes" among individuals. Such harmonic models often take names that include the word *pluralism* and offer relief from what ails traditional education by promising to foster *tolerance*. Pluralism and tolerance as goals, "Left" critics suggest, too often fall back essentially on deprivation models in different cloaks as they imply a sort of norm against which all else is deemed "different," but to be "tolerated."

The forms such models take in K–12th grade classroom practice are often embarrassingly shallow, ignorant of both the world of academic ideas as well as the worlds of lived experiences—they are what James Banks calls "teepees and chitlins" practices (1989). They render trivial various cultural formations and practices and continue attempts at defusing (repressing) anger and assimilating difference into structural norms by way of a new kind of "happy talk." "Everybody's beautiful in his/her own way," or "we are the world" can be heard humming just below the sound level. For example, in one elementary school I visited, a Christmas program was produced in which the children sang a variety of songs. Out of ten songs (performance of which included costumes and some acting), eight were traditional Christian songs, one was "Hanukkah Is Here," and the other was "Calypso Noel." I suppose the intent was to foster multicultural awareness and tolerance. How even this modest and misguided ambition would be realized within the clear centrality of an Anglo-Christian holiday and ceremony is beyond me. It was clear whose religious tradition set the scene for any others.

But even those practices that incorporate more critical interpretations of particular histories (of colonialism, slavery, misogyny, for example) into the curriculum, too often do so through unbelievable superficiality (e.g., history is still *told* as "the truth" or as mushy relativism), and through methodologies that might contradict the messages. Testing and grading have not changed so much, for example, despite the best efforts of texts for multicultural teacher education, primarily because the systems that demand them have not substantively changed. Indeed, most universities as well as schools expect to be able to report grade and test-score advances for students, grant-getting, credentialing, and publication advances for faculty.

A colleague who has worked for several years with teachers in schools through what might be termed "multicultural education workshops" offered these remarks about his experiences:

> I don't think there is any model of multiculturalism that I find especially compelling . . . and I don't know really what the term means anymore. In conversation yesterday, I found myself saying that I'll stick with the term as long as I think it has any political value . . . that

is to say as long as I think it might be used to motivate people to any kind of change, especially during this reactionary period. Teachers had smart things to say about a kind of multicultural bandwagon effect; [how it] tended to lead to sloppy cultural sensitivity in service, and a few minor curricular changes. . . . Of course, no one wants to talk about urban/suburban inequities, or, for that matter, the general [trend] towards defunding the system as a whole. In that regard, MCism is a nice distraction and good humored. But I don't know: it seems no better or worse than any other current slogan (outcome assessments, writing across curriculums, local control, schools within schools, etc., etc., etc.). Educational theorizing is going to have to get messily political I think. (James Hall, personal communication, June 28, 1995)

Many teachers are well beyond the shallow practices I critique in doing what they and others might be calling multicultural education. Less often are such sophisticated practices schoolwide. I am arguing, however, that the more rich and deep practices I read about and see teachers engaging could certainly be called cultural studies. As we will see, cultural studies, while encompassing multiple theoretical and intellectual approaches and agendas, nonetheless has an avowedly political agenda that has, so far, not been so easily diffused or defused. The diversity of its intellectual life enables it to adapt to local situations, while the commitment of its politics helps it to retain a critical distance for action. As we will also see, cultural studies, as with any intellectual trend supported by academe, is also in constant danger of being appropriated into the "teaching machine" (Spivak 1993) without changing that machine substantially. My hope is that its theoretical and political traditions will undermine appropriation such that, at least, no reactionary project can call itself cultural studies.

My characterization of the criticism of multicultural education is fast and vastly simplified, but suffice it to say for my purposes in this work, much of what has passed for multicultural education has lacked a thoughtful grounding in the controversies raging in humanities and social science departments of academia, or in the dialogues and conversations that generate life outside of schools, in neighborhoods and communities struggling to make livings and meanings of their own.

And, for that matter, academia is all too ignorant of both school and street-culture talk. Such ignorance both supports and is a part of the interpellation of academic intellectual life into the big "teaching machine," a machine whose parts depend on one another to function in the ways they do as a whole, but a highly contradictory machine—a corporate-style assembly line in which those at work in classrooms and offices, researching and writing, are isolated from one another, the larger institution, and the world beyond. We are isolated and thus highly seduced into concerns over narrow worlds of publication, internal debates, and promotion and tenure such that we are far too distracted to see, let alone deal with, the larger picture. The capacity to address the contradictions of an institution that offers degrees in discourses around social and cultural justice while at the same time functions to thwart academic freedom and free speech in its own communities is dramatically diminished. As such, my hope for a translated curriculum applies to the curriculum for professors as well as teachers and students at all levels of the educational enterprise.

Revisioning multicultural studies through the lens of cultural studies allows for such a broadening of possibility, extending the most critical and effective moments from the work in multicultural education. For example, cultural studies insists that any aspect of history be examined from multiple perspectives, but most particularly from the perspectives of those who were most affected, usually most victimized, by events, policies, and phenomena. Likewise, literature, popular cultural forms, and science are to be thought through particularities of context at the same time larger systems are compared. Such an approach embraces the notion of a cross-cultural "conversation" that neither reduces one culture to the concerns of another, nor proliferates into infinity the "multiplicities" or "pluralities" of human concerns.

Through interdisciplinary, cross-cultural approaches to studies—including studies labeled "Western"—such a conversation might be possible. For example, a class reading Melville might also read Toni Morrison's interpretation of *Moby Dick* in an article which is also about race, culture, history, and an intricate phrasing of the question "what and who is 'Western'?" (Morrison 1989). Indeed, I contend that encounters between cultures shape and transform those cultures, not so they all become the same, but such that neither exists as pure and unmediated—outside a conversation. That mediation is often expressed in literary works. A turn to cultural studies provides a useful frame for thinking about such a project, and hence, the subtitle of this book, a play on a statement by Spivak:

> The real problem . . . is that we live in a country which has plural-ism—the pluralism of *repressive tolerance*—as the *best* of its political credo. Most of us are not interested in changing our social relations, and pluralism is the best we can do. *Cultural studies into multicultural-ism.* (1993, 18–19, emphases added)

I want to imagine how the multiculturalism of "repressive tolerance," such as that enacted in the elementary school Christmas program, might move in the direction of cultural studies—a direction that insists on the grounding of historical specificities without insisting on a single way in which to find that grounding. Cultural studies might provide a frame that is at the same time better theorized (than multiculturalism's) *and* more sensitive to particularities of context.

Cultural Studies

To the extent that it makes sense to talk about origins, the contempo-rary configuration of cultural studies can be said to have been conceived in the 1950s in Birmingham, England by Stuart Hall, Richard Hoggart, Raymond Williams, and E. P. Thompson. All four were "extramural teachers," which meant that they were marginal to the academic centers in England, where they taught such courses as lit-eracy for adult working-class students. They were marginalized, in part, because none of the traditional academic disciplines fit cleanly into their interests. As such, they were thought of as lacking rigor, among other negatives. Cultural studies has since gained legitimacy in the British academy (Stuart Hall was given a chair in sociology though his academic degrees are in literature, and the Center for Contemporary Cultural Studies [CCCS] became well-established). But, in many senses, it continues to fight for full membership as England continues to undergo some identity crises similar to those of the United States, where we have best-selling books calling for "cultural literacy," for "opening" the "closed" American mind, and for a return to "the canon." There are other strands of cultural studies—Australian, American, and French, to name dominant others—which influence and converse with British cultural studies and with one another to varying degrees. For example, Stuart Hall draws on the work of contemporary French poststructural philosophers Foucault and Derrida in his most recent work, whereas earlier work was influenced by more structuralist theoretical perspectives derived from Marx, Althusser, Gramsci, and Frankfurt School critical theory. The structuralist influences persist though they are blended with poststructuralism now.

While there has been a cultural studies movement in the United States paralleling the British one, its status as a somewhat organized and recognized area of scholarship is more recent. One event marking a trend here was a conference called "Crossing the Disciplines: Cultural Studies in the 1990s," sponsored by literature professor Robert Con Davis and the Oklahoma Project for Discourse and Theory in 1990 at the University of Oklahoma. It is Davis's contention that "the study of [literary] criticism can profitably be situated as a part—and a leading part—of the study of culture. . . . In fact, a strong argument can be made that the texts we customarily call literature constitute a privileged site where the most important social, psychological, and cultural forces combine and contend." This has been a line of a number of British cultural studies scholars as well. Literature is only a part of what captures and constructs the popular imagination. Other (popular and "high") cultural forms are vitally important. (Literature and autobiography, however, are the focus of this book with my understanding of their partiality.)

Since the Oklahoma conference (and I'm not suggesting *because* of it) cultural studies has exploded on the U.S. academic scene. In 1991, Lawrence Grossberg, Cary Nelson, and Paula Treichler hosted an international conference called "Cultural Studies Now and in the Future" that drew around nine hundred people to the University of Illinois at Urbana-Champaign campus. Presenters and some other invited participants contributed papers that were later bound into a rather large anthology called *Cultural Studies* (1992). The editors introduce the volume as follows:

> The field of cultural studies is experiencing ... an unprecedented international boom. ... In the United States, where the boom is especially strong, many academic institutions—presses, journals, hiring committees, conferences, university curricula—have created significant investment opportunities in cultural studies, sometimes in ignorance of its history, its practitioners, its relation to traditional disciplines, and its life outside the academy.[1] (1)

Since 1992, when this anthology came out, cultural studies in the United States has only expanded. Academic departments by that name now exist in some universities. There are many more books in print with "Cultural Studies" in the titles, and there are a number of new journals. There are even a few journals now that are claiming affiliation with cultural studies in the field of education. Nonetheless, informed use of the term "cultural studies"—regardless of reference to British or other—is still a rare event in colleges of education. For this reason, despite the fact there are a number of essays devoted to framing the history and definitions of British cultural studies (Aronowitz 1993; Hall 1980, 1990, 1992; Johnson 1986–87; Nelson, Treichler, and Grossberg 1992; Grossberg 1993, 1995; Turner 1992), I offer my own summary, derived from my readings of those before me, to interested colleagues in education.

British Cultural Studies: A Brief History and Description

Originating texts, or what Hall calls the "original curriculum," include Richard Hoggart's *The Uses of Literacy* (1958), Raymond Williams's *Culture and Society* (1966) and *The Long Revolution* (1975, originally published in 1961), and E. P. Thompson's *The Making of the English Working Class* (1978, originally published in 1964), the last being a critique of Williams's work. These early texts built on the work of F. R.

Leavis in terms of his efforts to deploy literary criticism as a means of reading "social arrangements, the lived cultures and 'languages' of working class life, as particular kinds of 'text'" (Hall 1980, 18). While they utilized some of Leavis's notions of cultural critique, as well as Matthew Arnold's, they departed from these two in terms of partisanship and the fixing of *Culture* with a capital "C." Williams's work, in particular,

> shifted the whole ground of debate from a literary-moral to an anthropological definition of culture. But it defined the latter now as the "whole process" by means of which meanings and definitions are socially constructed and historically transformed, with literature and art as only one, specially privileged, kind of social communication. (Hall 1980, 19)

In *The Making of the English Working Class*, E. P. Thompson produced a labor history which challenged older versions by breaking with a limiting economic determinism and institutional perspective, and by going beyond a Leavisite elitist version of culture in favor of a notion of culture situated between "social being and social consciousness" (20). It also implicitly challenged Williams's somewhat evolutionary approach to culture in *The Long Revolution*. "Thompson insisted on the historical specificity of culture, on its plural, not singular, definition— 'cultures,' not 'Culture'" (20).

Another ground of contestation for British cultural studies was at the site of British sociology, which in the 1950s was "massively dependent" on American sociology (20). As characterized by Hall, American sociology was predominantly either Parsonian or structural-functionalist in methodology, and as such was incapable of dealing theoretically with issues of culture as conceived by the new cultural studies. It denied the category of contradiction in favor of such notions as "dysfunctions" or "tension management." It claimed no ideology and even disclaimed ideology as a sociological concept, except to attribute it to "totalitarian society" as opposed to the (non-ideological) "pluralist society" that was America. This polarity was advanced as scientific fact. "Culture" was dealt with only "within the terms of a highly pessimistic variant of the 'mass society/mass culture' hypothesis." Furthermore, the methodology it preferred was "modelled on a highly outdated version of the natural sciences, militantly empiricist and quantitative" (21).

"Schools of English and Contemporary Society" was Hoggart's lecture introducing cultural studies at the Birmingham Centre. It proposed two emphases for the program: (a) primary concern with neglected materials from popular culture and mass media, and (b) deployment of literary critical methods as an approach to reading such materials for their "qualitative cultural evidence" (21).

This lecture precipitated vigorous attacks by both the sociologists and the humanists. Sociologists, "while not concerned with such issues [as popular culture and mass media], reserved a proprietary claim over the territory" (21). The humanists

> regarded "culture" as already inscribed in the texts they studied and in the values of liberal scholarship. Anything more modern was, by definition, a sign of cultural decline and debasement. . . . They shared, in fact, with Leavis, the assumption that culture and democracy were unalterably opposed. (21–22)

Finally, by incorporating history and historiography into the sociological work of cultural studies, the dualism of literary versus sociological was broken down. Also, by performing historical analyses on the classic sociology texts themselves, thereby situating them outside of science and inside history, the field of sociology began to be appropriated from within. Through this process other neglected sociologies were turned up as well, such as German sociology (Weberian; hermeneutic approaches of Dilthey and Simmel) and American "social interactionism" (in the work of Mead, Dewey, and the Chicago School) (22–24).

For several years, a central and ongoing debate at the Centre and in cultural studies generally was over a perceived incompatibility between *structuralism* and *culturalism*. From its inception—with Hoggart's *Uses of Literacy* and beyond—cultural studies was concerned with the lived experience of real people. Yet, the problem with this perspective, structuralists claimed, was that the work attending to such concerns too often seemed to lack theoretical grounding. Such work ignored the larger conditions under which cultures were produced. The culturalists, on the other hand, were critical of the excessive determinism of the structuralists. Williams and Thompson, in particular, were concerned with the pessimistic outlook that dismissed any notion of human agency capable of resisting the power of history and ideology (Turner 1992, 11–13).

Structuralisms eventually entered the conversation at the CCCS as European works by Lukacs, Benjamin, Goldmann, Levi-Strauss, Barthes, Althusser, and Gramsci became available as English translations. Through these authors, theoretical turns were taken and explored with the growing sense that early conceptions of culture and ideology were oversimplified and undertheorized. As a progression of European structuralist theorists captured the interests of various scholars at the Centre, with each turn the debates over culturalism versus structuralism became more intricate. For example, the traditional Marxist base/superstructure metaphor became more and more radically revised to include interactions among all practices—economic, political, ideological, and cultural. Althusser's concepts of overdetermination and relative autonomy (1971) were particularly exciting for this movement. Nevertheless, the problem of human agency, insisted upon by culturalism, remained inadequately addressed by Althusserian theory. In particular, the solutions offered by structuralism seemed especially lacking. As Hall puts it:

> Its formalism and rationalism, its privileging of the highest levels of abstraction as the exclusive mode of operation of "Theory" with a capital "T," its obsession with epistemological issues, themselves constituted formidable barriers to the solution of problems which structuralism itself posed. (1980, 29)

The culturalism/structuralism split ceased to hold a significant place in the Centre with the introduction of the work of Antonio Gramsci. "Where Althusser's explanation implies that cultural change is almost impossible and ideological struggle futile, Gramsci explains how change is built into the system" (Turner 1990, 32). "For Gramsci, 'hegemony' is never a permanent state of affairs and never uncontested" (Hall 1980, 36).

While Gramsci "remains within the basic terms of a materialist theory" (36), Foucault's work represented for cultural studies tendencies to look beyond materialism to critiques of earlier semiotic models and appropriations of psychoanalytic theories. Hall's ambivalence is once again aroused by this theoretical turn as the problem of determination is repressed, while, at the same time, the problem of representation is reopened (37).

This has also proved a crucial opening for theorizing around gender and race. The impact of feminism in particular imposed a crisis on the CCCS in that questions of sexual difference are seen, in many senses, to precede social class differences. Certainly, social class (difference) is more complicated by its interactions with gender issues. Also, since the writing of Hall's 1980 essay, theorizing around race has entered cultural studies in a similar manner. All of this has required a radical rethinking of many theoretical perspectives and agendas for the Centre, with a concomitant need for redefining. As Hall explains with regard to the feminist break:

> We were opening the door to feminist studies, being good, trans-
> formed men. And yet, when it broke in through the window, every
> single unsuspected resistance rose to the surface—fully installed
> patriarchal power, which believed it had disavowed itself. . . . When it
> came to the question of the reading list. . . . Now that's where I really
> discovered about the gendered nature of power. Long, long after I
> was able to pronounce the words, I encountered the reality of
> Foucault's profound insight into the individual reciprocity of knowl-
> edge and power. Talking about giving up power is a radically
> different experience from being silenced. That is another way of
> thinking, and another metaphor for theory: the way feminism broke,
> and broke into, cultural studies. (1992, 282–83)

Defining Cultural Studies: Evasion, Necessity, and Constraint

In 1983, Richard Johnson produced his essay asking (and tentatively answering) "what is cultural studies, anyway?" (later published in the 1986–87 issue of *Social Text*). Many of the concerns with defining, and thereby possibly constraining and undermining cultural studies remain at this writing the same as they were in the beginning. Johnson writes:

> A codification of methods or knowledges (instituting them, for example, in formal curricula or in courses on "methodology") runs against some of the main features of cultural studies as a tradition: its openness and theoretical versatility, its reflexive even self-conscious mood, and, especially, the importance of critique. (1)

Critique in the cultural studies tradition has meant critique of the disciplines through "raids" (Hall 1990, 16) in which elements are lifted from areas such as sociology, history, anthropology, literary criticism, and philosophy—elements which are useful to theorizing culture and the movements and workings of power. What remains after these raids is rejected. As such,

> it involves appropriation not just rejection. From this point of view cultural studies is a process, a kind of alchemy for producing useful knowledge. Codify it and you halt its reactions. (2)

Yet, pressures to define are real. At the level of daily politics of colleges and schools is the need to attract resources for jobs and research. In terms of the larger political field, there is need for resources to challenge conservative assaults on public educational institutions, and "to decide priorities for teaching and research" (7). Johnson also sees a need for viewing cultural studies not as unity, but as whole for the purposes of "reforming the elements of different approaches [appropriations from the disciplines, and theories] in their relations to each other" (7).

Johnson suggests "strategies of definition" which would presumably maintain the integrity of cultural studies critique. His strategies are as follows: critique by defining (a) as an intellectual and political tradition, (b) in its relations to the academic disciplines, (c) in terms of theoretical paradigms, or (d) by its characteristic objects of study. He favors the fourth one. I will not elaborate on these for the reason that, in terms of the CCCS, the question of departmentalization (a kind of definition) has become a moot one since Johnson's writing of this. Under University pressure to be reabsorbed into the Department of English, CCCS managed a compromise whereby they became the Department of Cultural Studies. This meant creating and offering an undergraduate curriculum whereas before the Centre had sponsored only graduate students and provided only reading and research groups without formal classes (Turner 1990, 79). With the diffusion of their (still) small departmental numbers to preparing and teaching undergraduate courses as well as directing graduate students, it is feared that what was the CCCS will lose the powerful influence it has had on the international scene. As Turner explains, prior to departmentalization,

> it adopted a policy of encouraging its students to publish their work rather than produce assignments or even finish their degrees! While this did little for the Centre's "academic throughput figures," it did make the work visible, disseminating the fruits of its research and establishing the reputations of its students. (80)

The issue of definition is less settled elsewhere. Ellen Rooney (1990) suggests that research and practice in cultural studies might best survive the ravages of such groups as the National Association of Scholars (NAS) by emulating women's studies (with regard to their visible commitments and influences outside the university). She also asserts that, in order to retain its critical edge, cultural studies (in the United States) must resist the pressure to being incorporated as a discipline. If incorporated, it would "abandon its position as a critical reading of the traditional disciplines and of the disciplinary as such" (17). Rooney draws an analogy to the situation for cultural studies in the U.S. from the history of American Studies. Its having become an established discipline fragmented it politically such that "American Studies too frequently participates in the resistance to progressive work in the humanities" (18).

On the other hand, other scholars of cultural studies are concerned about such distancing from the traditional academic disciplines. Rooney interviewed Gayatri Spivak, who expressed such a concern:

> if one establishes an interdisciplinary space which does not engage with the most important arena (a silent, unemphatic arena) of warring power in the disciplines themselves, where the people who don't pub-

lish much, who don't teach very well, engage day after day, as with distribution requirements, let us say, if one doesn't budge them, but proliferates interdisciplinary, anti-essentialist programs, in fact one provides an alibi, once again, for the ruthless operation of neo-colonialist knowledge. (Spivak 1989, 133)

Should cultural studies in the U.S. retain its distance from "the disciplines," evading the "border patrol" that seeks to constrain by a strategy of define-and-conquer, and better avoid the risk of losing its critical capacity, *or* should cultural studies operate through "conversations" across and within, through self-critique, remaining within the traditional disciplines (where it has mostly been, de facto), and, perhaps, better avoid the risk of divisiveness and academic marginalization? Is academia even the proper place for the activist work of cultural studies to be centered? Given the political agenda of cultural studies alongside the pressures for (especially untenured) academics to speak and write primarily to other academics, this last question is provocative. Note the following comment by Jan Zita Grover in a discussion following her presentation at the Urbana Cultural Studies Conference:

I don't feel like I can do what I need to do inside the academy. That's why I am no longer there. And what I said at the beginning and lost as I got angrier (as I always do about the AIDS crisis in particular) is that students are not being in any sense prepared for what happens after they leave the university [i.e., they are not prepared to both act and do "brainwork"]. (1992, 235)

In this spirit, I too left academia for a year, with the thought of maybe leaving for good to do work that is more grounded in the material, less in the textual (if I may be permitted to make that distinction momentarily). My decision to do that, and then to return to academia, at least for a while, might better be the subject of another book. But I mention it here to provoke thinking otherwise than our "institutionalized selves" as possible ways of doing the work of cultural studies.

It is also relevant at this juncture to differentiate between the British and American *contexts* for cultural studies. Though many of us in departments of education are either unfamiliar, or just becoming familiar, with the histories and discourses emerging initially from Britain, those discourses have rather exploded in other academic departments. What does this mean for American cultural studies and the work it can do? Stuart Hall recognizes the phenomenon as a "moment of profound danger" for those of us involved in this work in the United States (1992, 285).

> I think of the struggles to get cultural studies into the institution in the British context, to squeeze three or four jobs for anybody under some heavy disguise, compared with the rapid institutionalization which is going on in the U.S. . . . Well, it would be excessively vulgar to talk about such things as how many jobs there are, how much money there is around, and how much pressure that puts on people to do what they think of as critical political work and intellectual work of a critical kind, while also looking over their shoulders at the promotions stakes and the publication stakes, and so on. (285–86)

The danger is, at least in part, that when the stakes are so high, when money, power, and prestige are rapidly changing hands, the movement might just be another venture "headed off at the pass" by appropriation and assimilation into the system, the "teaching machine." This is one of the profoundest and most discouraging criticisms of what has been called multicultural education, the very idea that I am suggesting be displaced by cultural studies. Such a displacement is worthless unless we determine never to lose sight of the tension between the intellectual work and the political work of cultural studies.

But even the first two questions raised about defining ourselves *within* academia are not so simple. Given the complexity of the situation whereby cultural studies scholars from many academic departments, with a tremendous diversity of interests, are increasingly being lumped together and charged with being "politically correct" dogmatists or, sometimes rightfully, with being obscurantist, the first two questions might not be about real options. That is, there are likely very few opportunities for cultural studies to departmentalize itself. Though there *are* departments of cultural studies now, they are not likely to become the norm for universities and colleges across the country. My own hope is that reduction to such an "either/or" (either we departmentalize, or we "raid" the standing departments from within) can be avoided, at least in some important respects. For that matter, one might hope as well that we need not define ourselves as *either* academics *or* "organic intellectuals" working outside the academy.

When we look at the public ("nonacademic") debates around multicultural education, the humanities, the canon, and "Western culture" that are directed at practices and curricula for primary schools through higher education, the problems for workers in cultural studies emerges more clearly in some senses. It becomes clear that our work is needed beyond academia as business-as-usual.

The "Culture Wars"

In the introductory chapter, I mentioned the centrality of the copy machine in the high school where I once taught. It was a place where teachers, and sometimes administrators, met more often than anywhere else to talk about issues, what we were teaching and how. And it marked a moment for me of recognition—recognition of the significance of publication as event, in this case the Hirsch and Bloom phenomenon of 1987.

Looking back through that moment, extrapolating further back to what was preceding, and forward to what came after, I want to suggest a recognizable trend over a relatively short span of time. In 1986 new demographic information about our cultural and racial makeup and the state of the "traditional family," poverty, and other items were big news (see, e.g., *Education Week*, May 14, 1986). We read statements such as, "California is already a majority minority." The news seems to have marked a crisis, inspiring waves of fear and dread among, especially, white Euro-Americans. Is it any coincidence then that, in 1987, Hirsch's *Cultural Literacy* and Bloom's *Closing of the American Mind* would become bestsellers in hardback, despite the often academic languages employed? And how, precisely, did those books become bestsellers? It has been suggested that the kind of money that backed them initially, and the kind of media representation both received, were instrumental in their monumental sales. One might reasonably ask: Who was afraid, and of what were they afraid? (And I'm not suggesting some conspiracy theory here.)

By 1989 a rage was exploding in the popular press, often coming from disgruntled academics, about the "tyranny of political correctness" rife on our campuses, and even sometimes in our schools (in the name of multicultural education). This explosion can be traced in the popular press as being most intense between the years 1989 through 1991. During that time, the term "political correctness" worked its way into our national vocabulary such that we now hear "PC" roll off tongues routinely, with little regard for the history of the meaning of the term. It has become just one more rhetorical device for not-thinking, for shutting down dialogue, the very thing the rage over it was supposed to counter. Or it has become a subject for questionable and derisive humor, as a book entitled *Politically Correct Bedtime Stories* exemplifies, itself a bestseller in college campus bookstores and beyond.

So, a reasonable suggestion is that the public discourse around current controversies over the humanities and school curricula in the United States was initially framed, to a significant extent, by conservative and neoconservative academics, including E. D. Hirsch, William Bennett, Alan Bloom, and to a lesser extent Lynne Cheney. (Lynne Cheney has since become increasingly vocal in a number of arenas.) This is not to say that they represent a monolithic position. Each of the above-mentioned speaks from a different notion of "the good," and what is considered "good" is key to their arguments about what the humanities are and what purpose they serve. The "humanities" that they criticize do not teach "the good" as they conceive it. For Cheney, the good is that which is "aesthetically pleasurable" (1989); for Bloom, it is that which is "true and eternal" (1987); for Hirsch, the good is what is shared in "common culture" and what is (thus) expedient for teaching (1987); Bennett's view of the good seems to be synonymous with what he considers to be Western culture—"civilization's best thoughts and finest utterances" (1984, vii). Similar stances are taken by educationists Diane Ravitch and Chester Finn with reference to secondary education (1984, 1985, 1987), and later by Ravitch with reference to higher education (1990).

Compelling arguments against such perspectives have come from a number of less publicly known critics (and herein lies the problem for cultural studies scholars as well—our work is too often not visible in the public domain), who also hold diverse viewpoints. Despite all the diversity, it is possible to see a major split between two rough categories of views: those who view, shall we call it, Western cultural studies as both having a discernable "essence" and as primary, and those who question such essentialism and/or the primacy of "Western" culture to study of the humanities.

Also at stake is the very definition of the humanities. Does it include the "social sciences" as well as the usual—art, music, literature, drama, etcetera? Many seem to agree that it does, though to widely varying degrees. A problem with this question, of course, is that what we call the "social sciences" is not clear either. According to Clifford Geertz in his article "Blurred Genres" (1983), just about everything can be thought of as text and can thus be interpreted via literary criticism. If this is so, then it would seem that nothing is completely outside the domain of the humanities. Geertz writes:

> The great virtue of the extension of the notion of text beyond things written on paper or carved into stone is that it trains attention on precisely this phenomenon: on how the inscription of action is brought about, what its vehicles are and how they work, and on what the fixation of meaning from the flow of events—history from what happened, thought from thinking, culture from behavior—implies for sociological interpretation. To see social institutions, social customs, social changes as in some sense "readable" is to alter our whole sense of what such interpretation is. (1983, 31)

Critics of this idea complain that such an orientation to "the disciplines" reduces to absurdity the possibility of coming up with a core curriculum for humanities studies in the United States. Ironically, many advocates of multicultural and afrocentric education are likewise committed to the installation of something like a core curriculum—if not a national one, at least a statewide one. (See, e.g., Ali Mazrui's recommendations for New York State Public School history curricula, the Portland "baseline essays" for history that is afrocentric, and standards

developed for the National Center for History in the Schools.) These
are not, however, the sorts of core curricula conservative critics of afrocentrism, multicultural education, or "textuality" as an intellectual and
instructional perspective have in mind. Indeed, Lynn Cheney heads the
battle against the National Center for History standards (*NCTE
Newspaper*, April 1995). Ravitch and Finn, who advocate the institution
of a national core curriculum for secondary school humanities, also
advocate the strict separation of those disciplines (history and literature, primarily) in high school teaching (1984, 250–57). This is clearly
a position defined in opposition to the notion of "blurred genres." The
desire for a core curriculum along with the rather convergent questions
and answers about what constitutes "the good" represents the most
striking difference between the two "rough categories" of viewpoints—
a difference which most often generates an impasse to discussion about
the subject among critics, both "left" and "right," and even within the
"left" itself.

The Hirsch, Bloom, Bennett, Ravitch, Finn, and Cheney contingent
share at least the assumptions that "the good" is to varying degrees
knowable and is so in a fairly "objective" sense. They are, one might
say, "Western essentialists." But any who desire a pre-set curriculum
that promises to deliver "the truth" in history and literature, including
multicultural or afrocentric education advocates, are likely falling into
an essentialist trap. Critics of this sort of essentialism doubt the possibility of an objectively knowable good that can be prescribed for all
curricula in the humanities. Interpretive approaches that most offend an
essentialist standpoint involve not only the disruption of a canonical[2]
curriculum by inclusion of, for example, culturally diverse literatures,
but also the historicization of canonical works. Historicizing literature
reveals the contexts of its production (or even the notion that its production might *have* a context!). Glimpses at the circumstances and
consequences of literary productions strip away a sense of naturalness to
social/cultural formations that the productions represent. The works in
question (canonical or not) and the cultures they represent are revealed
as *impure* . . . in many senses of that word . . . hybrid. From this standpoint it becomes difficult to mark off and fetishize something called
Western culture, or *any* culture. (Re)interpretation is at the heart of the

critical stance against essentialism that has as a pre-set definition for what is called Western culture the "best thoughts and finest utterances." These critics (let's say for now, the "anti-essentialists" . . . though this language, too, becomes problematic, as we shall see in the next chapter) see reinterpretation as the only way change (social or individual) takes place, as well as the only way the world is understood (Rabinow and Sullivan 1987, 27). The possibilities for multiple interpretations suggest an impossibility for certainty that shatters an essentialist structure.

The essentialist view assumes that Western culture (or African, or Native-American, or virtually any other) exists and can be studied and understood in isolation from other cultures. This notion is exemplified by Bennett when he writes, "in studying other cultures it is best to begin with a thorough knowledge of our own" (1984). The degree of naiveté expressed within such a notion is of the order of one who misunderstands the irony of Martin Mull's *The History of White People*. This sort of thinking plays out at the level of practice when, for example, at one state university in northern Louisiana, an institution that is only about 7% black in a city that is 50% black, a course proposed on the history of black education was rejected on the basis that it "singles out one group and thus promotes race hatred."

The historiographical assumptions behind this essentialism are at the same time *monumental* (with regard to the grand American System) and *antiquarian* (nostalgic for a mythical past) in nature. In contrast, a *critical* historiography is one which links the past to the present through continual reinterpretation and by working from standpoints which challenge dominant narratives. Such historiography is advocated by the American Council of Learned Societies, an organization that has been harshly criticized by Cheney and others (Watkins, 1989). The "danger" of this approach is not only that it challenges traditional humanities curricula, but that it can call into question a "whole way of life" (Raymond Williams' definition of culture). Such a view of history and the humanities strikes essentialists as ideological and biased (which of course it is, as is any perspective), and as wanting only to tear down. Again, this is an issue similar to that of who is "other." It is about notions of difference. Critical reinterpretation looks for differences as much as similarities/commonalities. The critical historian would ask,

"How can one even begin to arrive at opinions about the good society or culture without bases for comparison and argument?" This exposes a contradiction in an essentialist position unless one admits to believing, as does Allan Bloom, that "the good" has already been determined for all time—it is transhistorical. Most don't go this far—at least not consciously or publicly. For to admit to this belief is to rather automatically exclude a multiplicity of cultural groups which constitute American society.

Ravitch, Finn, and Hirsch defend themselves to critics who claim their project is elitist. Their defense is basically that they propose the same education for all—that everyone has a right to become knowledgeable of "our cultural heritage," with culture defined by Matthew Arnold, and interpreted by essentialist curriculum designers. What they apparently fail to recognize is that *definition* of culture has historically excluded so many from the domain of legitimated knowledge. The point is not to replace in the curriculum that which has been generated by an Arnoldian view of culture with another canon—another list of "greats." Indeed, it is critical that we know the forces that have shaped us, and those forces include patriarchal and racist ideologies. Nor is the literature of the "traditional curriculum" to be discarded as rubbish; it (mostly) is *not*. The point is that a liberal education is one that provides a passage to transformation of ideologies rather than mere transmission.

Criticisms of so-called political correctness, of multiculturalism, and of the humanities became, in those years roughly 1988 to 1991, increasingly strident, and seemed to be erupting from the same section of the gallery. At a conference held by the National Association of Scholars in November 1988, those assembled were exhorted "to redeem American higher education from intellectual and moral servitude to forces having little to do with the *life of the mind* or the *transmission* of knowledge" (emphases added). Such forces were characterized as consisting of academic radicals who engaged in "oppression studies." Other examples of comments made were: "the barbarians are among us. We need to fight them a good long time. Show them you are not afraid; they crumble," and "Say to the feminists, 'what do you mean by separate courses? You have no methodology.' When you lose,

make them state their agenda to the world. They haven't got the guts to state it, and you'll beat them that way" (cited in Rooney 1990, 15). This meeting was attended by such media figures as Boston University president John Silber (often cited in the work of Ravitch and Finn) and Jeanne Kirkpatrick. Use of the term "barbarian" as opposed to "civilized" is found repeatedly in the Ravitch, Finn, and Fancher book (1984, 82, 240), where barbarians are apparently those who do not have anything that can be called "the humanities," lacking "culture" in the Arnoldian sense.

Yet, at certain points conservative criticisms such as those of Ravitch, Bennett, Hirsch, and Bloom, converge with more radical critiques. Many are concerned in some senses about the alienation that is symptomatic of what is sometimes called the failure (or incompletion) of modernity—the fragmentation that devalues a liberal education, one rich with the insights provided by deep involvement with history and literature. A significant difference in the perspectives of the above-mentioned conservative critics and my own is in an orientation toward language, toward textuality and interpretation, that recognizes the power of language to shape subject positions—the ways in which dominant narratives are "written" and taken up—and how, therefore, tradition is necessarily translated across time. Hence, in order to be able to read the world well one must be ready and able to reread it within ever-changing contexts. Translating (textual) tradition involves the reading of "old" and "new" texts together in an intertext that is simultaneously faithful to the old and available to the new. I know of no better way to honor tradition or a "life of the mind."

How do different language use, different discourse, the different texts we read and the different ways we read the same texts, shape us differently? Imagine, for example, three rough categories of discourses about multiculturalism, cultural studies, diversity, or any other similar terms as coming from 1) academia, 2) institutions of schooling, and 3) popular media. Which words does each category use to describe these ideas and phenomena?

In academia I hear (and sometimes write) about: *subject positions, the decentered subject, hybridity, postmodern subjects, politics of identity, politics of difference, history as narrative, truth as constructed, post-positivism, decon-*

struction, ideological apparatuses, and so on. From what I can see in and about institutions of schooling the most common terms are: *learning styles, self-esteem, attitude, values, history as truth-telling, cultural differences, cultural understanding, building bridges, achievement, gender-role identities, bilingualism, prejudice, identity (as fixed),* and so on. In the popular media I hear (either the terminologies themselves or veiled references to the ideas): *political correctness, demise of Western culture, angry white males, male-bashing, dead white males, rewritten histories* (as critique of especially afrocentrism, for example), *affirmative action, quotas, race and I.Q., hate speech [versus] freedom of speech, balkanization, fragmentation, official language, assimilation = Americanization, Euro-American = Western,* etcetera.[3] What do these differences in language use do to our perceptions of one another and ourselves? What do they offer us in terms of understanding one another and ourselves? Many of us cross these categories in our work and lives. How do we resolve those categories?

Finally, in looking at these debates, the problem for cultural studies emerges not so much as one of its definition or "academic codification" as it is a problem of combatting what Wilson Harris calls an "illiteracy of the imagination" (1989). That Ronald Reagan was known as "the great communicator" elicits the following response from Harris:

> So many things are eclipsed, so many things are lost sight of, and masses of people respond because the way he communicates allows him to operate within a certain sort of frame which seems to simplify everything and to make it easy, so that there is no difficulty in comprehending what is being said. (16–17)

It is an illiteracy of the imagination among Reagan's supporters, Harris suggests, that explains Reagan's persuasiveness. It stems from a comprehensive inability to read outside a uniform frame, a uniform kind of narrative. "No wonder," Harris writes,

> we live in a world of such fanaticism. If we have cultures which are locked into certain functions, which read the world only in one way, then fanaticism grows out of that, terror grows out of that—a total

refusal, a total difficulty to read the world in any other way, to make any other kind of adjustment. (18)

Being locked into "block functions," as Harris puts it, prevents our recognition of the deep and intricate ways in which social, cultural, and other marginalizations are played out in real bodies. If we learn to believe that our lenses are universal and fixed, we can not translate, hence we cannot connect with one another nonviolently. Essentialisms are manifestations of block functioning, though we might find it necessary at times to deploy "strategic essentialisms" (Spivak 1989, 125–26). Indeed, essentialism and block functioning are never perfectly escapable.

Moving multiculturalism into cultural studies means, inescapably, to move through theory as a necessary "detour on the way to something more important" (Hall 1991, 42). Theory that links local political goals to larger worlds of texts and bodies and back again, endlessly, . . . is about reading well, about being disabused of our own "abused record with no choice but to repeat itself at the crack [of the phonograph]" (Morrison 1992, 220).

3

Theory and Difference

Marginality, Essentialism, Translation, Love

THIS CHAPTER is divided into separate sections with subheadings for *marginality*, *essentialism*, *translation*, and *love*, but it should be understood that these separations are, in important ways, artificial, as the categories function through and within one another both in terms of my vision of them and of my writing. The separations are intended to act as markers calling attention to key issues as they figure most prominently here. It should also be noted that the four subheadings are not the only problematics that emerge in this writing. They simply serve as organizing principles. These theoretical categories have been set up but not completed or enclosed in this chapter. These constructs become more fully developed as they are viewed in action—that is, as they are engaged in the literary and autobiographical readings that come later.

Identity and the *Currere* of Marginality

The ways in which marginalized groups, individuals, and ideas come to be marginalized in a given culture, society, and/or place has much to do with what is considered to be knowledge and who is considered to possess it—who is perceived as knower and who is perceived as known. Clearly, education is deeply implicated in these processes. The literary and autobiographical works examined in this book confront the notion of marginality from different racialized and gendered standpoints. I use the term *confront* to emphasize the problematic nature of marginality as it appears in these works. In these texts the marginalized are, in many senses, in a position to know more about the group, culture, society, or other forces that keep them far from the center than can members of that center know about the margins (Freire 1970). Likewise, marginal aspects of even those who are in the center in the broadest sense, are the aspects of self through which they gain a metaperspective or distance from self. This is because the margin must "know" the center in order to survive, but the reverse is not true to the same extent. Yet neither margin nor center exists as such without the other. Hence, there is an infusion of each in the other. I refer to this idea as the *currere of marginality.*

Currere, as William Pinar explains (1975), is the Latin root of the word *curriculum*, which literally means "the running of a course" (a race, the course of one's life, etc.), and its study "involves investigation of the nature of the individual experience of the public" (400). It is by the experiences and ideas through which I am marginalized, or through which I *choose* to dwell or travel in margins,[1] that I experience the public as a distinct member. And it is from that experience that I gain multiple perspectives around notions of self, other, and society as both separate and connected.[2] Pinar elaborated an autobiographical method on the basis of his interpretation of *currere* (1975). Because *currere* is the Latin root for *curriculum*, *currere* of marginality takes a double meaning. It is both a particular approach to autobiography that is focussed on marginality, and it is about a curriculum of marginality. With both autobiography (the written stories of our lives) and curriculum, stories are constructed and told. Often those stories spring from a dominant or unitary narrative. As individuals, when such stories contradict our experience, they create or feed neurosis. The "unique outcomes" (White and Epston 1990) that make up our experience are left disturbingly unstoried. Stories for such unique outcomes offer us alternative ways of constructing and performing meaning in our lives, which affect the ways we read texts and the world. Finding and writing these stories is what the approach to autobiography I call *currere* of marginality is about. This is part of what I mean by "choosing to dwell in the margins." As described here so far, it differs little from Pinar's original method of *currere*, which involves a four-step exploration into the temporal and conceptual and its relation to the evolution and education of the Self (Pinar 1994). Perhaps the only difference that will emerge is the self-conscious way a *currere* of marginality reconnects the individual to the social and cultural margins. This is what grounds it in cultural studies.

A curriculum of marginality is also about excavating excluded stories, or storying "unique outcomes," in the interest of constructing and performing alternative meanings and ways of being in the world. To the extent the social-communal layer of marginality (discussed further below) is repressed and denied in school curricula, pushed underground in favor of "happy" and "safe" reading and writing, the dominant stories that support social neurosis and psychosis (apathy and violence) cannot be challenged. Chapter four begins with a story about an elementary education-methods class I taught. The projects we produced were aimed at developing not only a method, but also a social studies curriculum by specifically focussing on what was omitted from elementary-school social studies textbooks. Our approach was based in cultural studies and is an example of building and learning within a curriculum of marginality.

Marginality both as theoretical concept and embodied existence is a source of big trouble. It "lives" within the very language/world that makes it necessary and that it must oppose. Paradoxically, it must oppose the notion of opposition. Frequently, marginality is placed in binary opposition to centrality or dominance, where it is further reduced to social categories such as race, class, and gender with little or no regard for the intersection of these categories with smaller group and individual contexts. Social theories and institutions as well as philosophical writings based on the logic of binary opposition are ill-equipped to deal with the nuances of these (non)categories and their implications for the production of subjectivity. *Literature* is often the only written source of assistance and encouragement for one who wishes to think about these issues in a multidimensional way.[3] Ralph Ellison, in his *Shadow and Act*, echoes these concerns in the context of expressing his reasons for writing fiction:

> Unfortunately many Negroes have been trying to define their own predicament in exclusively sociological terms, a situation I consider quite short-sighted. Too many of us have accepted a statistical interpretation of our lives and thus much of that which makes us a source of moral strength to America goes unappreciated and undefined. (1953, 16)

As alluded to before, marginality in this writing is not only about the socially and culturally marginalized. Marginality can be viewed from at least two perspectives or layers: social marginality and individual marginality. The socially marginalized refers to lives which lie outside the dominant culture (the center). While I am aware that race, class, gender and other labelled categories are social, historical, linguistic and cultural constructions rather than natural or universal ones, at this particular historical juncture it seems accurate to refer to the margins of larger United States society (the socially marginalized) as, in part, people of color, economically deprived, physically challenged, homosexual, and female. Still, it can be argued that everyone is marginal in at least some aspects. The way we attempt to define ourselves has a great deal to do with who or what we attempt to define as "other" to us. And it is at the frontier between this self and this other (these selves and these others) that our own individual marginality lies. For example, if I situate myself as a white, middle-class woman, then anyone who I situate as non-white, non-middle class, and/or male would be an other to me. But, I may also exhibit characteristics that are traditionally thought of as masculine, I may come from a working-class background, and my physical appearance, manner of speech, and behavior may be "racially ambiguous." Therein rests part of my marginality in what might be called the individual layer. This particular example of individual marginality also illustrates, albeit simplistically, the interaction between social and individual layers in that the individual layer differs from the social layer by virtue of ambiguity around categories that define the social layer. In other words, there exists something beyond these two layers, an interactive space where these layers enfold one another, which reveals the leakiness of boundaries between different forms of marginality and between margin and center. There are *many* margins and they carry a range of psychological and material effects that are not equal in intensity or force. As individuals, societies, and ecosystems, our *identities* are constituted by our margins.

The problem with defining margins and, by default, centers as such, is that in doing so we are stuck in a language of oppositions whereby the only option for (linguistic, and hence often material) change is to move from one pole to the other, a complete reversal, or to merge the two in dialectical synthesis, obliterating differences and flattening out the cultural landscape. Either the insidious structure of hierarchy is maintained or the integrity of individual difference and autonomy is endangered. While it is sometimes strategically valuable to maintain a binary opposition, or to subject it to dialectical synthesis, often a more desirable state of affairs could result from deconstruction of that hier-archical system—and I speak here of deconstruction as set forth by Derrida. Spivak explains this notion in the context of the feminist con-cern with the public-private split (opposition):

> The shifting limit that prevents this feminist reversal of the public-private hierarchy from freezing into a dogma [synthesis] or, indeed, from succeeding fully [reversal] is the displacement of the opposition itself. . . . The opposition is thus not merely reversed; it is dis-placed. . . . The peculiarity of deconstructive practice must be reiterated here. Displacing the opposition that it initially apparently questions, it is always different from itself, always defers itself. It is neither a constitutive nor, of course, a regulative norm. . . . It is in terms of this peculiarity of deconstruction then that the displacement of male-female, public-private marks a shifting limit rather than the desire for a complete reversal. (1988, 103)

As such, what I have called the interactive layer of marginality is some-times a dialectical synthesis of social/individual or even larger, social/community/individual, and sometimes a deconstruction of those layers, which undermines claims to a "positive" stable identity for either self or other, margin or center.

Deconstruction, Dialectics, and "Identity"

What is the difference between a deconstruction and a dialectical synthesis of the layers of marginality? There are, of course, many different accounts of "dialectics." I am basing my discussion of the difference between dialectics and deconstruction on a particularly lucid account of Marxist dialectics by Bertel Ollman (1986). In the paragraphs that follow I go into perhaps more detail than such an interlude in my arguments should warrant. There are three reasons for this: first, the differentiation is complex; second, I have been unable to find this explicitly done elsewhere; and third, such a discussion deepens the discourse about marginality and essentialism.

A dialectical approach assumes that the processes by which events take place are knowable and, somehow, sensible. Thus, it must assume a certain transparency of language (through to reality). Analysis or investigation that proceeds through dialectical thinking is indeed complex and dynamic. In that sense, it is not mired in chains of certainty or predetermined outcomes. However, in a total sense, such analysis can proceed only through a kind of faith in the knowable—an epistemological faith. Dialectical thinking, as it is most often characterized in contemporary theory, is dependent on a notion of structure which presupposes a center of meaning of some sort (even those structuralist theories that regard social formations as a "decentered" structure). "This centre governs the structure but is itself not subject to structural analysis (to find the structure of the centre would be to find another centre)" (Selden 1989, 87). A dialectical approach depends on conceptualization as direct connection to the real, thus giving rise to the possibility for synthesis or incorporation. It is a movement between concepts in search of the knowable. The concepts with which it deals are necessarily assumed to be opposites, at least in key aspects. This would imply that to some extent the concepts (in this case the three layers) can be thought outside one another. (Derrida's notion of the supplement in deconstructive thinking denies this possibility.)

Dialectical thinking is predicated on what Serres calls the "ordered structure." In one essay, he begins his account of this with a quote from La Fontaine's "The Wolf and the Lamb" parable: "The reason of the stronger is always the best" (1982b, 15). The ordered structure, like the positioning of the wolf and lamb (and shepherd and dog) along the running stream, "designates a set of elements provided with an ordering relation" (16). This can be diagrammed as three points (a, b, and c) on a line with a direction (irreversible). Each point is either preceded or succeeded, or both, by another point. No point can precede or succeed itself, so the relation is irreflexive. From this model of the ordered structure one can define processes of dominance ("strength"), reason, causality, hierarchies in general. "The order of reason is only a particular exemplar of order in general. And this has immense consequences" (17). The operation of the ordered structure proceeds through a series of trials in which the first task is to establish responsibility. To win in this trial it is necessary to "play the role of the minorant" (20)—to demonstrate injury or victimization. The game is a never-ending dialectical process. "Stable structures and dialectical processes are inseparable" (21).

Given this characterization of dialectical thinking, I do not dismiss it as an important strategy for approaching certain types of problems, especially at a theoretically "local" level. As Guattari explains:

> Certainly, in the field of social ecology in particular, there will be times of struggle in which all men and women feel a need to set common objectives and act "like little soldiers"—by which I mean good activists. (1990, 7)

However, such a synthesis inevitably gives rise to new contradictions, and this is where a deconstructive approach to thinking and reading may provide relief. (It should be noted, ironically, that setting up this comparison as an essential opposition is "antithetical" [a term that introduces another ironic turn] to the spirit of deconstruction.)

Deconstruction is based in rereadings—the refusal of final meaning (or synthesis), even momentarily. It proceeds in search of a space between concepts—a marking of the unknowable. Realist representation that can emerge from dialectical thinking and synthesis is viewed as an illusion of presence. Not unlike notions of power for Foucault, for deconstruction meaning is not inherently a problem until it becomes (viewed as) static, and asymmetric in its stasis. As such, a deconstructive approach may sometimes be inappropriate to particular problems of an immediate, daily, or local nature (problems that Jacques Daignault refers to as difficulties) because of its infinite deferral and lack of closure. That is, to think of it as a "method" which is applied to difficulties whereby "solutions" are perpetually deferred can result in a nihilism and passivity.

On the other hand, a deconstructive approach to the problem of marginality in three layers could indeed have strategic interventionary value for specific (i.e. local and particular) problems in that it allows for a play of reversals among those layers, as long as the reversals are not made static. Sometimes, even for difficulties, solutions need to be temporarily deferred. Deconstruction also acknowledges the extent to which layers of marginality cannot even be thought outside or apart from one another, at the same time they are not collapsed onto one another. For a dialectical approach, a kind of sublation among layers is the goal. Such an approach is unable to take into account breaks and discontinuities in meaning.

A deconstructive approach to the three layers would seek spaces between, by virtue of these breaks and discontinuities in meaning, which defy categorization (knowledge), but which nonetheless mark a persistence that is unsayable. Its expression in words (or otherwise) is not possible by any direct approach. Such expression is found in literary works, for example, where direct and positive categorization of "messages" or "morals" cannot be drawn, but where, perhaps, a sensibility remains—where a good reading leaves in its wake the trace of cross-cultural experience, a partial translation that is never final but always open to rereading, reinterpretation, retranslation. It is not an attempt to subsume through synthesis, incorporating differences and discovering oneself in every other.

Deconstruction is a conscious acknowledgment of the ordered structure and an attempt to subvert it—an attempt which is ultimately

impossible in any total sense. In terms of issues surrounding multiculturalism, racism, sexism, the value of deconstruction over dialectics is
its "self-conscious" recognition of the ordered structure and the way in
which the structure itself produces, necessarily, victims. Possibilities
and visions for processes/movements capable of minimizing violence
and victimization seem most plausible through this awareness that
works to keep power and meaning in motion.

Finally, the *idea of identity* almost "begs the question" of whether or
not to approach it dialectically or deconstructively, as these approaches
ultimately signal particular orientations toward identity and subjectivity in their very constructions. That is, by some interpretations,
Derridean and other poststructuralist approaches deny the very existence or meaningfulness of "identity" because there can be no unitary
self by these accounts. (This problem will be further addressed in chapter five with respect to autobiography.) Another example: both
Merleau-Ponty and Levinas argue "that the subject can never grasp its
own act of grasping" (Taylor 1987, 204). As such, Merleau-Ponty
posited a "dialectic without synthesis" to replace the "bad dialectic
[which] is that which thinks it recomposes being by a thetic thought, by
an assemblage of statements, by thesis, antithesis, and synthesis" (cited
in Taylor, 79).

Paulo Freire could be said to operate through dialectical thinking in
his approach to the oppressed (the marginalized), and thus to identity.
According to Freire, the marginalized, or the oppressed, are the only
ones who can understand the full significance of oppression, and are
hence the only ones who will have the vision and the strength to eliminate it. The greatest obstacle to their accomplishing this feat, he says,
is that the oppressed "are at one and the same time themselves and the
oppressor whose consciousness they have internalized. The conflict lies
in the choice between being wholly themselves or being divided . . ."
(1970, 32). This idea is an example of what is known in dialectical
thinking, as it is laid out by Bertel Ollman (1986), as the "interpenetration of opposites." However, according to Friere, once this process
begins there is a danger of complete reversal, due, in part, to internalization of oppression and the consequent identification of oppressors as
embodying what it means to be human. Another danger comes from

attempts (by whom is not clear—perhaps, for example, by individually marginalized people at the social center?) to facilitate the activism of the oppressed through the use of "monologues, slogans, and communiqués" rather than dialogue. This is an "attempt to liberate the oppressed with the instruments of domestication" (Freire 1970, 52).

While Freire's sense of marginality as expressed here most closely corresponds to what I have called social marginality, part of his concern is similar to Spivak's "deconstructivist" warnings about being subsumed within the very discourse being opposed. The difference is in Spivak's insistence that one can never oppose a discourse from a position entirely outside it. In so doing, Spivak is able to encompass a broader sense of marginality to include the interactive layer. That idea is illustrated (and was alluded to earlier in this writing) by the very use of the word "oppose" for a "project" that wants to displace binary oppositions (Spivak 1988, 106, 108, 110). This problem, however, is not a contradiction so much as it is a paradox. (A paradox, as I use the term here, is a problem that does not require—indeed cannot have—a solution. It requires deconstructive reading.) Displacement is not the same as elimination. As Russell Ferguson explains:

> The intent is not to create a new center of authority based on a spurious unity of the marginalized, but rather to open up spaces for new ways of thinking about the dynamics of cultural power. (1990, 9)

Indeed, marginality in all its layers is constituted by encounters. The social margins result from encounters across *differences between* (in terms of race, class, gender, nationality, sexual orientation, etcetera)— encounters that often have necessitated one-way translation by the marginalized of those who suppress and oppress them; that is, "translation with a master" (Rajchman 1991, 7). Encounters across *differences between* transform *all* of those involved in some ways. When translation takes place *without* a master, the transformations that take place can set cultural power in motion, blurring the boundaries between margin and center. (More about this a little later.)

Individual margins can be thought of as encounters across *differences within*—differences generated by socially and culturally produced psyches within "singularized" subject-positions. Clearly, these margins emerge in the context of the social, but are not, in many respects, predictably determined by social structures, in part because the social structures are themselves highly contradictory. My margins are precisely those areas in which I am unpredictable, a surprise. When that unpredictability becomes a surprise even to myself then I have been set up to learn. I discover, and begin to story, my "unique outcomes." When those margins are set in the context of their interactions with the larger (social and communal) margins, the readings required become more complex, richer. I learn through good readings of the world (and that includes readings of myself), just as good reading is reading that is situated to allow for the "surprise of otherness" (Johnson, B. 1987, 15). Good readings are those that operate at some conscious level through all three layers of marginality.

A reading that sets up the conditions for a knowledge-within-difference would proceed through some degree of awareness regarding collective and individual histories of the movement and ambivalence of desire, of exploitation and privilege, and of the possible relationships among these. (Autobiography is one place to explore those relationships.) For example, William Pinar's essay "Understanding Curriculum as a Racial Text" (1993) is both itself such a reading and at the same time a call for and a description of the conditions for eliciting such readings from teacher educators, teachers, and students. In this essay, Pinar explains how, psychoanalytically, the repression of African-American history, literature, and culture can be understood in terms of attempts at American identity formation and stabilization. Such an identity can only be sustained through a kind of willful ignorance that distorts and deforms at the level of the *individual and the social* both European-Americans and African-Americans alike. Such a national identity can only be sustained through deployment of a "border patrol" between center and margin.

Desire operates through this labor (of sustaining national identity) from within a history that lives in the present, not unlike the lie that is told and goes out of control, in snowball fashion, requiring constant re-creation to protect not only the perpetrator, but all who were taken in. The desire itself (to perpetrate a lie, for example) is what must be explored. What is needed, Pinar suggests, is a kind of social psychoanalytic therapy to expose the lie and save the subject—to de-center then "re-center" the subject on the basis of cross-cultural encounters that assist the continuous (re)constitution of it. That subject is himself. It is also the rest of us, as citizens of the United States. Exposure and exploration of the lie and what drives it presents a surprise of otherness when I discover that as a European-American I am being constituted also by that which is African-American, that this interpenetration lives and moves through a collective unconscious and memory of which I am part and from which, at the same time, I differ. Now I can read in a new way. Ground is provided for a new assemblage and *literacy of the imagination*.

The Essence of Essentialism

The problem I refer to—margins and centers, frontiers, boundaries, outsides and insides, the places of reified (and re-reified) structures—is about the necessity for coming to terms with difference and otherness. As Mark Taylor reminds us, "The history of society and culture is, in large measure, a history of the struggle with the endlessly complex problems of difference and otherness" (*Altarity* 1987, xxi). Learning is about difference and perception. And difference that is perceptible is necessarily concentrated at the boundaries, fluid and dynamic though they be, between margin and center. Thus, a society that values learning also values and loves and listens to its margins. Yet too often, to be marginalized is already to be situated in a kind of "double bind" with respect to the centers of society. That is, the socially marginalized are expected to adopt and function within a cultural "memory" that is not truly their own at the same time they must struggle if they wish to be included in that society.

At the same time that the margins are posed with a double bind, their questions and other responses to the center take the form of another kind of double bind—a kind of chiasmus to the double bind of expectation/exclusion imposed on the margins by the center. Margins, being both advantageous and dangerous territories, ask us to abandon an ostensibly rationalist discourse by posing questions and responses to the center in the form of mixed messages that say "I am this," "Don't label me as this."

For example, in challenging the common wisdom about race among white people as well as among her peers in the literary community, Zora Neale Hurston frequently played with stereotypes and clichés about race. She does this in an essay called "How It Feels to be Colored Me" published in *World Tomorrow* in 1928 (examined by Barbara Johnson in 1987). Hurston divided the essay into small separate parts and responded to the question differently in each part. By so doing she, at times, appears to give contradictory answers to the question as she reverses and rereverses clichés about race. Her "answer" comes, therefore, from the piece as a style. Hurston's reversals play between herself as essentially black (different from you, white person) and essentially nothing (the same as you, white person). Johnson's speculation is:

> In the first essay, Hurston describes the jungle feeling as an art, an ability to feel, not a reversion. In the second, the jungle appears as a result of "strain." In the first, Hurston can proclaim "I am this"; but when the image is repeated "you are that," it changes completely. The content of the image may be the same, but its interpersonal use is different. . . . The difference between difference and sameness can barely be said. It is as small and as vast as the difference between "like" and "as". (1987, 177–78)

This call for abandoning a rationalist discourse is often heard through literature, poetry, and art—symbolic arenas that have historically been more often excused from the "responsibility" of rationalism. Through such literature, the problematic of an antiessentialism/essentialism binary is exposed and, as I see it, calls up two notions of essentialism: essentialism as it is typically used in a pejorative sense—that is, one that absolutely prevents translation (the signifier becomes the signified); and another that ambiguously simultaneously demands and rejects translation—"translate me" or "I am this, understand me" and at the same time "do not translate me" or "do not label me as this." (Translation will be discussed further below.)

49

The first sort of essentialism is based on the notion that identities of persons and things are stable and definable according to transcendental essences and/or standards of judgment. The second is a destabilized essentialism that is locally and strategically deployed as resistance to the first as well as to "terrorism" generally. The difference, as expressed by Diana Fuss, is that the first type of essentialism is "inherently reactionary—inevitably and inescapably a problem or a mistake" (1989, 20). The second type when deployed "may have some strategic or interventionary value . . . the radicality or conservatism of essentialism depends, to a significant degree, on *who* is utilizing it, *how* it is deployed, and *where* its effects are concentrated" (20, emphasis in original).

The case of Susie Phipps in Louisiana (in 1982) in conjunction with much of civil rights legislation provides an example that demonstrates the political, social, cultural, and psychological problematics coming out of the antiessentialism/essentialism binary opposition. Susie Phipps contested her legal definition as black, which was arrived at by conformation to a Louisiana state law (1970) that asserted that anyone who had "one-thirty-second black blood" was indeed black. This was to be determined by genealogical records which, in Phipps's case, indicated that a great-great-great-great grandmother had been a "Negress and a number of other ancestors mulattoes, quadroons, and octoroons" (Dominguez 1986, 2).

The trial involved expert testimony from anthropologist Munro Edmonson who argued on Phipps's behalf that by virtue of the way genes are "shuffled" before birth it is at least theoretically possible for one to inherit all genes from just two grandparents. Furthermore, he cited "modern genetic studies [that] show that blacks in the U.S. average 25% white genes and that whites average 5% black genes, and that by these statistics, using the one-thirty-second law, the entire native-born population of Louisiana would be considered black!" (2). (How these statistics were arrived at raises other interesting questions that I am not now prepared to deal with.) Though Susie Phipps lost her case, Louisiana overturned the controversial law in 1983. But the question of legal racial identity remains, though now at least ostensibly for different purposes. With the hard-fought battles over civil rights legislation, legal racial distinctions have been deemed necessary in order to insure equal protection under the law. The contradiction that arises is one where legal distinctions on the basis of race may both limit *choice* at the same time they enhance it in other ways.

This case demonstrates the demand for deconstruction (a kind of "acting out") of that binary which opposes essentialist definitions of race (as in blood, for example) to "antiessentialist" claims of uncertainty. At the same time, it points to the second form of essentialism/translation, understood dialectically as the ambiguous and shifting one, as politically strategic for the marginalized. Replacing what is dynamic with static essences (or, for that matter, static "antiessences" that claim to know the essence of essentialism) is a characteristic of modern social and economic structures. It is what Milan Kundera calls "totalitarian kitsch," which is, he says, "the absolute denial of shit," the expression of a desire to reach "an agreement with being as such" (*Unbearable Lightness of Being*, 1984, 248, 249). It "deprives people of memory and thus retools them into a nation of children" (*The Book of Laughter and Forgetting*, 1981, 235). Robert Boyers writes in a letter to Kundera, "Collective activity inevitably entails parades, slogans, and the belief that one is right. So you suggest. To oppose totalitarianism is to ask questions and to refuse to become a model of anything, not even of dissidence" (1985, 231).

But, if democracy is possible it should by its very definition resist totalitarian kitsch. It is difference that puts the pressure on governments to live up to democratic ideals. And kitsch, as conceived by Kundera, is the absolute denial of difference. But how does one "deconstruct" such a binary when deconstruction itself is often touted as a paradigm of antiessentialism? Herein lies another aspect of the double bind presented to us all by the margins.

This double bind has been articulated and explored extensively by such literary figures as Milan Kundera, Zora Neale Hurston, Toni Morrison, Wilson Harris, and Ralph Ellison. They all deal either explicitly or implicitly (or both) with notions of double binds and the "schizophrenic" insight that they induce. I see an interesting linkage between some of the language and literature of schizophrenia and the characterization of the reader of literature in a state of engagement with a text. The engaged reader is said to experience a dissolution of the reading self—a "moment of dispossession of the reading ego: as separation of itself from itself" (McCormick 1988, 177). Of course, those who are "clinically schizophrenic" probably suffer a "dispossession of the ego" which goes far beyond the momentary.

Gregory Bateson, in his *Steps to an Ecology of Mind* (1972), included an essay "Toward a Theory of Schizophrenia" (201–27) in which he reflects upon his work with schizophrenics. He notes that schizophrenics spent their childhoods caught in a double-bind sort of logic. That is, they received incessant, inescapable, contradictory messages with regard to their own behavior and feelings from one or more significant family members. The "way out" for these people is to develop different systems of logic in order to deal with the situation and to translate from other systems to their own. Such logic is often circular and rich in metaphor. The difference between this metaphor use and ordinary metaphor use, Bateson suggests, is that schizophrenics use "unlabeled" metaphors in the form of distorted syllogisms. For example: "Men die. Grass dies. Men are grass" (205).

My purpose in drawing analogies among a debilitating schizophrenia, the marginalized, and the reader engaged with a text, is by no means to imply the existence of a pathology to be exorcised from the latter two, or to trivialize the tragic suffering of many deemed schizophrenic. It is simply to illustrate that when one is confronted with a challenge to one's logical system, such as what often occurs with reading and learning and living in the margins, one is forced to compensate, and does so through a schizophrenic moment. There is also a decontextualization about schizophrenia that seems similar to those aspects of reading in which the reader is submissive to the text. Again, they are but moments for the reader in which s/he is confronted with difference, challenged to be creative of new systems but temporarily relatively unanchored to history. As Alan Nadel explains, while we read,

> we may even rest on one set of connotations, but we do so very tentatively, for the pleasurable compact of reading is that we are always open to moments of acquisition and surrender—in which we recover and discard implications brought to the surface by the text. (1988, 51–52)

For Wilson Harris, the process of writing is also schizophrenic:

> the unity or density of original expression in a work of profound imagination, is paradox; it is both a cloak for, and a dialogue with, eclipses, of live "otherness" that seek to break through in a new light and tone expressive of layers of reality. Sometimes this combination and breakthrough . . . is schizophrenic. (1983, xvii)

I wonder if it is these rebellions against logic, this playfulness, the schizophrenia in us all that allows for the construction of new "schema," configurations, categories, via something like "unlabeled metaphors." For Deleuze and Guattari there exist "positive schizophrenic lines of escape" (1983, 363), which I interpret to be similar to this state of reading/learning/engagement/dispossession. The problem with the "sick schizo" arises, they say, when s/he is "effectively neuroticized" (363), paralyzed by the double bind. Bateson notes that psychiatric institutions are often themselves productive of the double bind (1972, 225). Likewise, I would argue, other institutions and the theories that produce and are produced by them can be. I see theory based on the movement of difference as providing a "line of escape," whereas much social theory within a privileged rationalist discourse attempts to enclose us in the double bind by telling us that our experiences and feelings are insignificant. Resisting from the margins, we can avoid that trap, and often do so through literature, poetry, art, storytelling, ritual, popular culture.

Translation and Tradition

Translation (without a master) is a vital concept and capacity to the project of creating an antiviolent curriculum.[4] It applies to multiple levels of the curriculum: selection of content (or, I prefer, "learning trailheads"), method of instruction, curriculum construction ranging from micro to macro levels. Translation—as an idea beyond the usual linguistic sense, and including words in the body and the body in words, words across discourses or disciplines, across cultural and his-

Susan Huddleston Edgerton

torical experience—has increasingly attracted my attention for its implications for learning and teaching. Because it is so vital and so rich an idea, I want to carefully explore translation in its own right before explicitly connecting it to curriculum.

Translation in this writing emerges as a composite notion from my readings through several authors (e.g., Derrida 1985; Rajchman 1991; Murray 1991; Niranjana 1992; and Serres 1982). For these authors, translation includes but goes beyond the purely linguistic categories set forth by Roman Jakobson. Those are: intralingual translation, or paraphrase; interlingual translation, or translation in the most common sense; intersemiotic translation, in which, for example, verbal signs are reencoded in nonverbal sign systems (1959, and cited in Derrida 1985, 95). In going beyond, Michel Serres writes of translations among the disciplines of literature, philosophy, and science that call into question the whole notion of separate "disciplines" (similar, in this regard, to cultural studies). John Rajchman (1991) theorizes a "translation without a master" that is a kind of cultural translation attuned to the politics and power relations of translation. David Murray envisions a cultural translation as something that is almost always possible, but always problematic, undecidable, and dynamic (1991). He describes the devastation of those forced to translate *with* a master—in this case indigenous peoples of the Americas. Jacques Derrida writes of the problematics of translation as being the problematics of the difference between signifier and signified—which is also "undecidable." Because this difference is impure, he prefers a notion of transformation to translation: "a regulated transformation of one language by another, of one text by another" (1981, 20). Henry Louis Gates shares Derrida's notion of translation as transformation but "translates" it to accommodate his African-American literary theory. For Gates, the texts in which he is interested demand constant retranslation, or at least bitranslation, just as the hyphen between African and American suggests a doubling (cited in Fuss 1989, 82–83). For Douglas Robinson (1991), translation that is good is embodied, somatic. Good translation is both an act of love and impossible, but necessary, suggests Spivak (1993). Shoshana Felman writes of the translation of memory in the writing of history. Tejaswini Niranjana notes the connection of translation studies to the

54

concurrent rise in colonialism and anthropology (ethnology), and suggests a new mode of translation as an "act of resistance" (1992, 84) involving the "re-writing of history in the post-colonial period by reading against the grain of hegemonic representations" (84). All of these approaches to translation, and translation studies, speak to the cultural studies curriculum.

For Serres (1982), a major (global) problematic involves finding passages between the sciences and the humanities. These passages exist, he contends, but they are not as simple as they have sometimes been made to be. Knowledge from all domains exists only as local pockets, or islands or spaces. The problem of these spaces has been repressed in favor of time which, ordered linearly, can be contained in an ordered structure ("ordered structure" being a structure sustained by global, unitary, and/or dominant narratives). The spaces of knowledge are local, not global, between which passages exist—but these passages are not generalizable. Spaces are disorderly multiplicities that resist a totalizing and linear history (1982b, xiii).

These passages or translations are found and demonstrated not through similarities, metaphors, or analogies but through formal operations of translation (translation as a mode rather than a specific act) whereby fundamental structures are found to be "isomorphic." That is, Serres explores the identical workings of the ordered structure (dominant narrative of an era and place) in different domains. For example, the industrial revolution provided the dominant narrative of an era, and that narrative was felt, reflected, and produced in all disciplinary and institutional domains. Hence, Serres suggests in his essay "Turner Translates Carnot" (1982, 54–62) that Joseph Turner's paintings *demonstrated* the second law of thermodynamics (entropy increases; the idea of increasing disorder or randomness), the same law that also emerged from the work of engineer Sadi Carnot. Writes Serres of Turner's painting *Rain, Steam and Speed: The Great Western Railway* (exhibited in 1844):

> Fire, the new history, passes like a thunderclap over the green water where a boat rocks. . . . The fusion of work in the real world. Always the object, always matter. . . . Man has constructed a thing-nature.

The painter makes one see the entrails of this thing: stochastic [random] bundles, dualism of sources, winking fires, its material entrails, which are the very womb of the world, sun, rain, ice, clouds, and showers. Heaven, sea, earth, and thunder are the interior of a boiler which bakes the material of the world. At random. (59–60)

Zola's texts provide another example as "the narrative does not function like a motor, it *is* a motor; thermodynamics is part of its very textuality" (xxxvi). Science, literature, philosophy, and myth of a period are equivalent cultural formations, according to Serres. Consequently, models of knowledge can be read to function in the same way across domains. Still, such connections are not obvious and require what Serres calls "rigorously disordered" readings.

This sort of translation can occur across layers of marginality (which also function across domains within dominant narratives of a time and place) and does so in certain literary works. For example, as Francoise Lionnet suggests, Zora Neale Hurston's autobiography *Dust Tracks in the Road*

> amounts to autoethnography, that is, the defining of one's subjective ethnicity as mediated through language, history, and ethnographical analysis; in short, that the book amounts to a kind of "figural anthropology" of the self. (1989, 99)

Hurston's autobiography translates across domains of literature, history, and anthropology, and it does so through both layers of marginality: social, through the categories of race and gender, and individual, through Hurston's simultaneous claims and disclaimers around those social categories.

Translation, in Serres's sense of it, is similar to the inter, or more accurately, antidisciplinarian efforts of cultural studies. His method for locating isomorphisms between different fields (or spaces of knowledge) is at the same time historical, literary, and anthropological; his analysis is philosophical, particular, and social. As the editors of his book of collected essays, *Hermes*, explain:

> if the separation of knowledge into regions, formations, or disciplines is no longer applicable, then knowledge must be reformulated on new

bases, new practical and theoretical operators must be discovered, and new operations must be defined. As we have seen, Serres calls these operations, interference, translation, distribution, and they all converge toward the idea of communication. (1982b, xxxv)

It is his notion of communication that links his specific notion of translation described above to that of other theorists here. For Serres, communication is contingent upon exclusion—not the result or demonstration of a dialectic movement between opposites. Fluid movement across boundaries without obliterating boundaries (margins, differences) is paradoxically hostile to communication and necessary for it. That is, there must be difference, the "excluded third man" ("parasite," "noise") in communication. It is what the communicators (interlocutors) team up against and try to destroy. Communication occurs in the search for sameness but it is necessarily a reaction to and against difference. As such, communication always risks violence (toward that which it excludes).

But translation is not reducible to communication. We do it when we are "alone" with our memories. The term *communication* also implies a kind of transparency of meaning-exchanges across difference that *translation* does not. One does not expect a translation to be complete or perfect. Indeed, it is, and has historically meant (since the sixteenth century), *transformation* (Makaryk 1993, 216). However, communication, or some degree of transmission of meaning, creation of meaning, is a vital part of the chain of translation. The final arbiter of the quality of a translation is located in its reception as meaning, and in its consequences. This is not to say that all memories, all human translations, must be articulated as speech or writing to be received or to have consequences. The work of memory and translation within a single person is received, in a sense, by those who *witness* something of that person's life—the way one lives a life.

Perhaps translation, given that it is always partial, can serve as an approach to communication that is not based in a desire to eliminate the noise of otherness. The notion that translation can take place presupposes some common meaning—some "common sense." Rajchman advises, "If it is sense that translation preserves, where there is translation, there can be no altogether new sense. There is always some sense in common" (1991, 6). Yet, too often the translations that take place in institutions called schools is such that the "common sense" ("common culture") is attributed only to a single dominant cultural identity. This is translation *with* a master, or translation in which meanings embedded in the discourse of a dominant narrative are privileged. This is certainly true of any form of "cultural deprivation" theory—theories which both explicitly and implicitly have pervaded social science discourses, imperial and colonial discourses. Despite good intentions, it is also true of those multicultural models or approaches that fail to recognize the complexity of difference and the production of subjectivity through the subtle, multilayered workings of asymmetric power relations. "Conversely," Rajchman continues, "translation without a master would be the art of breaking with those with whom one nevertheless identifies, while exposing oneself to the singularities of those one nevertheless tries to understand" (7).

Translation without a master is a two- (or multi-) way process. As Murray points out with regard to early encounters between aboriginal Americans and whites in the United States:

> In a situation of dominance, the cultural translation is all one-way, and the penalty to the subordinate group for not adapting to the demands of the dominant group is to cease to exist. Knowledge of the processes of this translation, though, must be repressed by the dominant side, in favour of a reassuring image of mutual intelligibility which does not register as significant who has had to "translate". (1991, 6)

This assumption of the transparency of language, this "unspoken belief in the isomorphic relationship between language and reality" (Greenblatt 1976, 572), is precisely the trouble with an ideology of positivism which has such a firm grip on current theory and practice in the curriculum field and in education generally. Rajchman asks:

> Can there exist a common sense, a public, or public space—a glasnost—which is not identified with a single tradition, or with a single way of classifying the plurality of traditions, but which is so divided

up that each tradition remains exposed to the singularities of the others, and of those yet to come? (1991, 6)

Such translations within the multicultural curriculum need not succumb to the criticisms of those who fear the "loss" of "Western culture and/or tradition." Tradition in such a new assemblage, contrary to accusations by some critics of multiculturalism, is not tossed out; it is *rearticulated,* reinterpreted, eventually reterritorialized (a continuous cycle); it is translated. Encounters among positions in the margins and the center result in such rearticulations of traditions—rearticulations that initially de-territorialize elements of the old. Just as the margins are simultaneously advantageous and dangerous positions, so is this de-territorialization. De-territorialization, as explained by Guattari, is a breaking up into singularities, it is ruptures of meaning, and it constitutes existential territories that have "always sought refuge in art and religion" (1990, 6).

> Each of the existential territories . . . exists . . . as a precarious, finite, finitized entity for itself; it is singular and singularized; it may bifurcate into stratefied and death-laden reiterations; or it may open, as process, into praxes that enable it to be rendered "inhabitable" by human projects. (8)

Such "human projects" become reterritorialized, transformed by cross-cultural imagination as, for example, in literary allusion—which is "to translate out of time" (Nadel 1988, 49). Allusion is a linguistic expression of encounters between, as in the case of postcolonial Caribbean territories, the traditions of colonizer and colonized. Or allusion can be a linguistic expression of encounters between the contemporary or popular and the traditional. It is a rereading of tradition in new contexts. It is the writing and rewriting of history. It is translation as an act of resistance. The paradox of tradition, Nadel indicates, is that "when we deal with the concept of tradition, we see that only its own manifestation can alter it" (1988, 30). In elaborating on the implication of allusion (in Ellison's *Invisible Man*) for "translating tradition," Nadel argues that the artist must . . . both invoke and overcome his or her historical sense. He or she must know the difference between the past and the present so well as to be able to afford not to know it. . . . Tradition, for Eliot, means the manifestation of the past in the new. (29)

It becomes a "revisionary repetition" (Moreland 1990, 4).

Nadel's theoretical use of literary allusion as a kind of revisionary repetition resonates with other theorists of the margins: Harris's development of "cross-cultural imagination," Lionnet's appropriation and extension of Edouard Glissant's "metissage," and Gates's "signifyin'." For Harris, forgotten pre-Columbian traditions return in his novels to interact with traditions brought by the Western colonizer, and the encounter produces a revisionary moment. He writes that within each of his novels

> there are different texts playing against each other, as much as to say that if you were to have a profound, creative democracy, you must have various texts playing against each other in such a manner that the tradition comes alive so marvelously that one begins to break the apparition of tyranny, the habit of conquest. (1989, 27)

Lionnet retains Glissant's notion of metissage in French rather than translating it to English (as "half-breed" or "mixed-blood" or "creole") as, in French, its meaning does not carry the negative connotation of the English translations. Metissage involves the braiding of "cultural forms through the simultaneous revalorization of oral traditions and reevaluation of Western concepts" (4) for the purpose of recovering unwritten pasts. It parallels

> the Greek art of metis [which] is an art of transformation and transmutation [alchemy], an aesthetics of the ruse that allows the weak to survive by escaping through duplicitous means the very system of power intent on destroying them. (18)

This evokes notions of the "trickster" and "signifyin'" as explained by Gates with reference to African-American literary theory, and which can be seen in the works of Maya Angelou and Zora Neale Hurston, for example. "Signifyin'" involves repetition and reversal of an idea—a chiasmus—which is carried out so as to "constitute an implicit parody of a subject's own complicity in illusion" (Gates 1987, 240).

The concepts developed by Nadel, Harris, Lionnet, and Gates will be more fully explored through literary readings in the next chapter. (Lionnet also provides autobiography theory which is useful to my project in chapter five.) I mention them now in the interest of elaborating a theory of marginality which is wary of the dangers of thoughtless essentialisms at the same it insists on the possibility for dynamic self-creation for the margins through translation and love.

The case of Susie Phipps illustrates one-way translation imposed on the margins from the center. "Ironically, the 1970 Louisiana law was enacted to supersede an old Jim Crow statute which relied on the idea of 'common report' in determining an infant's race" (Omi and Winant 1986, 162). However, this case represents faulty translation on three levels: (a) it represents an attempt to impose a language of scientific rationality on situations where multidimensional aspects of human experience are at play and at stake, (b) given that its authors buy into a scientific rationalism, they misread or fail to read scientific understandings, in this case, about recombinant DNA, (c) there is an attempt to make the local the global. It is translation *with* a master in that boundaries between margin and center are rigidly defined on the basis of a "purity," and that purity operates in only one direction—from center to margin. As such, the center is clearly defined as only that which is in no amount "other." The margins are left to fend for themselves out of a neglect that is sometimes benign, but more often not.

To communicate (to know), to translate (to attempt to know), is always to risk killing. Communication *and* translation are exercised in the attempt to eliminate the noise of otherness, to exclude, to marginalize, both symbolically and literally that which paradoxically forms a necessary backdrop for that same communication—that is, something against which exists the need to communicate. But maybe that violence can be best resisted (minimized) if communicating discourses (essentialisms) are localized journeys traversed in love (listening). The margins, like the Creoles of Louisiana, are local phenomena.

The particular historical relations of diverse cultural groups in a particular locale carry immense import for the processes of translation which continue to shape subjectivities for a region. It is in this sense that the cultural studies curriculum need attend to the notion of place. For translation to be a truly two-way process, local historical circumstances (relations among cultural groups of a place) have to be excavated and acknowledged. For even those who are relatively new to a region are affected by the region's history as well as by the specific histories they bring with them. Indeed, this movement constitutes new encounters which continue to shape the character of local and national cultures. These encounters cannot be explored outside a deep listening among and between marginalized and dominant groups. Such listening is, inherently, a part of translation that is a two- (or more) way process.

The pedagogy that I seek attends to the identity politics of individual student experience of literature and life, without collapsing under such politics to new "atheoretical" essentialisms. Translating the curriculum involves recognition and honoring of the isomorphic functioning/movement of events across disciplines, of local contexts of knowledge, of the "ecology of mind" (Bateson 1972) and body in classrooms and communities. Translating the curriculum also means translating the tradition of literacy constrained within block-functions (one that produces unitary readings of the world) to *literacy of the imagination* (literacy based in understanding of the significant linkages among language, the body, and the world). The deconstruction, dialectic, and translation that must take place in the classroom is situation specific, as is all ecological thinking, and as such, must fall back on questions of judgment. Judgment not based in love can only give rise to terrorism.

Love in the Margins

I begin this section with two quotes that represent a spectrum of love inclusive of mind and body, eros and agape, and something else beyond those dualisms. Perhaps that space beyond, explored differently by Michel Serres and Zora Neale Hurston in these quotes, could be referred to as "eco-erosic" love.

> Love has just been defined as an intermediary. It is neither a god nor a mortal, neither rich nor poor; it occupies the middle spot between

knowledge and ignorance. Love can be thought of as being among the fuzzy subsets. He is the included third. He is between. (Serres 1982a, 246)

And,

> She was stretched on her back beneath the pear tree soaking in the alto chant of the visiting bees, the gold of the sun and the panting breath of the breeze when the inaudible voice of it all came to her. She saw a dust-bearing bee sink into the sanctum of a bloom; the thousand sister-calyxes arch to meet the love embrace and the ecstatic shiver of the tree from root to tiniest branch creaming in every blossom and frothing with delight. So this was a marriage! She had been summoned to behold a revelation. Then Janie felt a pain remorseless sweet that left her limp and languid. . . .
>
> Oh to be a pear tree—any tree in bloom! (Hurston 1978, 24–25)

I write about a problem that has no solution other than love—and that is no solution because it resists the framework that anything called a "solution" requires. Not being "rational," love is well suited for dealing with the call to abandon the privileging of certain rationalist discourses. This love that I speak of is also listening—listening on many perceptual levels. Listening, as a part of language, is itself marginalized by so much philosophical writing that privileges the saying aspects of language (Fiumara 1990). Zora Neale Hurston loves us with her novel *Their Eyes Were Watching God* at the same time that she makes demands on our rationalist conditioning (with regard to double-binds, for example). She teaches us to listen. Michel Serres does the same.

With regard to my earlier positioning of female (which includes feminist perspectives and notions of the "feminine") in the margins of larger society, and my emphasis on love as integral to the workings of all the other oppositions operating within this text, I would like to preface my discussion of love with some notes about the connection between love as agape/eros and notions of masculine/feminine. Again, stressing my intent to avoid successful reversals (new essentialisms), I should perhaps clarify my use of the term "feminine" and thus also "masculine." Every man and every woman possess characteristics from both of the cultural categories feminine and masculine so that what are considered feminine and masculine are not coexistent with female and male respectively or exclusively. Yet "feminine" perspectives toward love are mostly marginalized in the philosophical literature, particularly in Western philosophy and theology. It is the "feminine" conception(s) of love, therefore, on which I wish to focus.

In my search for meaning in the idea of love I have examined some of the historical discussions stemming from my own "Western Judeo-Christian" cultural heritage (Plato, the Disciple Paul, St. Augustine, and finally Freud were read via Donnelly, French, Kristeva, O'Donovan, Soble). As several of the sources I consulted point out, such discussions are rich with possibilities, but they are largely lacking with regard to female/feminine perspectives. For female/feminine perspectives I have turned to a contemporary feminist theological interpretation of the Christian concepts of agape and eros (Donnelly 1984). My thesis (and Donnelly's as I read her) is that a "feminine" conception of love is one that does not hierarchicalize, and thus artificially split, agape and eros—a hierarchy which necessitates dualistic thinking with regard to mind and body, spirituality and sexuality. Donnelley and others call it "radical love" (30–34).

Agape refers, historically, to selfless love—especially the sort of love that is said to exist between God and human beings, but also within some forms of human friendship. It is considered to be the highest form of love in much of Christian (male) theological literature. Eros involves, but is not limited to, sensual, sexual and/or romantic love between human beings. Both terms have, however, been variously interpreted over time. True to Derrida's insistence on the indeterminacy of origins, contradictory readings of early usages of these terms abound. The opposition deconstructs itself when looked at historically.

Both eros and agape were concepts articulated by men. Plato spoke of eros, the disciple Paul spoke of agape. Erosic love for Plato was desire—love, and the search, for what was lacking. Plato separated mind and body within eros by differentiating between a raving or vulgar eros (body) and a sublime eros (mind). Thus, for the philosopher, love involved lacking and seeking beauty, truth, the good. Freud's notion of the libido (which is only male) is Plato's eros (Kristeva 1987,

59–82). St. Paul first announced agape as a sort of three-tiered plan for moving the concept of love away from eros and desire and passively under the thumb of the Father/God who bestows it. He emphasizes first, God's disinterested love for man, second, His sacrifice of the Son to prove it, and third, the importance of loving one's fellow man, including (especially) enemies and sinners as proof of allegiance to the Father (139–50).

Alan Soble interprets erosic love as being "property-based and reason-dependent," one in which we appraise the worth of the "object" to be loved, and agapic love as love which bestows value on the loved one regardless of prior properties (1990, 12). According to Soble, Eric Fromm sees mother love as agapic (unconditional) and father love as erosic, whereas Irving Singer considers all parental love erosic (13). Soble's definitions point to male imagery for eros and female for agape if one takes "property-based" and "reason-dependent" to be characteristics of modern patriarchy, and nurturing to be a "feminized" concept.

St. Augustine, like Plato, divides love on the basis of mind (spirit) and body while introducing the notions of sin and shame (O'Donovan 1980, 10). In the scheme of St. Augustine, women had little to say or offer as they were viewed as virtually all body with no mind or spirituality, and limited souls (French 1984, 107). With woman as body and man as mind, the (one-way) translation in Christian thought to woman's love as erosic (erotic) and man's love as agapic was easy. Both Plato and St. Augustine saw mind and body as separate and hierarchicalized—a dualism that has since proven vicious, but which is still very much in place in what has been called "Western rationalist masculine discourse."

Is another hierarchy emerging with these notions of feminine and masculine? Only in a limited sense, I think, because as stated before I do not believe these categories are natural, let alone restricted to associations of feminine to female and masculine to male. The limited sense of hierarchy I present here is an example of strategic use of fluid essentialisms. It is an inherently unstable one in that concepts/categories of feminine/masculine are historically and culturally defined moment to moment, and as such are synchronically, diachronically, and linguistically unstable. With this and my female status in mind it should come as no surprise if my arguments and discussion favor a feminist standpoint. I do not claim innocence, but neither do I apologize. Spivak speaks of this issue as follows:

> By pointing attention to a feminist marginality, I have been attempting, not to win the center for ourselves, but to point at the irreducibility of the margin in all explanations. That would not merely reverse but displace the distinction between margin and center. But in effect such pure innocence (pushing all guilt to the margins) is not possible, and, paradoxically, would put the very law of displacement and the irreducibility of the margin into question. (1988, 107)

A "feminine" complete reversal of the agape/eros hierarchy is a problem no less than the "masculine" version. The problem for everyone is the same insofar as an incomplete reversal or displacement is the goal. The ways to approach that problem are different—different broadly for masculine and feminine standpoints and different particularly for each individual. Still, I would argue for the existence of a certain advantage for the feminine standpoint through what I have called a *currere of marginality* (writing histories, autobiographies, and curricula against the grain of cliches and dominant narratives). The feminine standpoint in which eros (or feeling) is often allowed to supersede agape (rationality) is a marginalized standpoint in Western market society. (Although true agape is marginalized as well . . . a kind of pseudo-agape prevails—what Donnelley calls "sloppy agape" [1984, 20].) As expressed earlier, those coming from marginalized standpoints are typically more driven to deal with other more dominant standpoints and thus reach broader understandings encompassing multiple possibilities . . . or, go mad. This is why I feel some comfort in referring to the nonhierarchicalized yet noncontradictory conception of eros-agape as feminine.

It is through the multiplicitous experience of an entity, idea, or concept—both in mind and body—that we come to know it antiviolently. "True love" for anyone or anything comes from both mind and body, selflessness, and a kind of selfishness. I conceive of this selfishness as one where the lover attempts to soak up as much experience of the other, the loved, into the self as possible, though not in an intrusive sense, and not in a self-obliterating sense (both violent). It differs from pure agape (altruistic, selfless love) in that it involves more of an emotional investment and risk of rejection. But in order to truly be established such that it can grow and evolve it cannot be rejected—it must be reciprocal, the lover must receive a "return" on that emotional investment. Otherwise it never goes beyond agape, which by my interpretation of agape, need only be a one-way affair (as in "love your enemies"). This is not to say that agape is an inferior form of love—just that agape is neither superior, isolatable, nor is it all there is. I am also suggesting that displacement of these hierarchies is more easily associated with the feminine at this particular cultural moment, since such a standpoint could be conceived of as displacement of at least three oppositions: masculine/feminine, agape/eros, center/margin. The displacement or deconstruction of hierarchicalized love, I believe, is found in the idea of transference love—transference that is peculiar to the pedagogical situation. An explanation of this follows.

The pedagogical and psychoanalytic *risk* of love, transference love, is the displacement or deconstruction of hierarchized love (as in, for example, agape vs. eros, or love of others vs. love of self) and is a prerequisite for translation without a master. The implications that psychoanalysis holds for pedagogy are suggested by the significance of love to both. Henceforth in this writing love functions as an analogy for teaching/learning at the same time that it is often, as in psychoanalysis, more than an analogy; it is a very real and necessary condition for the pedagogical situation. This (transference) love "occupies the middle spot between knowledge and ignorance" (Serres 1982, 246).

Love (in the sense of "in love") effects a stifling of imagination (as in "love is blind") at the same time that it totally disrupts. It is a dangerous moment at the same time that it renews. "One speaks [of love (one learns; imagination returns)] only after the fact" (Kristeva 1987, 3). It subverts and problematizes language, providing an opening for translation across differences. It makes one unique and special (particular) at the same time that it blurs boundaries between self and other. Fear shares its symptoms. Indeed, love is "fear of crossing and desire to cross the boundaries [margins] of the self" (6). And, like learning, it is schizophrenic.

> In love "I" has been an *other*. That phrase, which leads us to poetry or
> raving hallucination, suggests a state of instability in which the indi-
> vidual is no longer indivisible and allows himself to become lost in
> the other, for the other. Within love, a risk that might otherwise be
> tragic is accepted, normalized, made fully reassuring. The pain that
> nevertheless remains bears witness to this experience, which is indeed
> miraculous—the experience of having been able to exist for, through,
> with another in mind. (4, emphasis in original)

Like learning/teaching, these are dangerous territories, disruptive,
unsettling, risking blowing apart all that is official or certain. Love and
learning are marginal passages. Love (learning) calls into question the
very notion of identity. Kristeva suggests that love dissolves "the limits
of one's own identity." At the same time it tests the "referential and
communicative power" of language to reach across this uncertain border (2). These are two quite different points—love both joins us (limits
vanish) and separates us (language stops working). What *do* we mean by
"love"? Searching the question reveals a "linguistic profundity," love
which is "solitary because incommunicable," is nonetheless translatable. Versions of love (languages of love) "commune [only] through a
third party: ideal, god, hallowed group" (3).

Can a classroom be one such third party, political problematics and
all? Kristeva writes:

> Love probably always includes a love for power. Transference love is
> for that very reason the royal road to the state of love; no matter what
> it is, love brushes us up against sovereignty. (9)

Transference takes place through a granting of authority by the
analysand (student? teacher?). We ask our students to "suspend disbelief" in our competence. We ask them to grant us authority. It is we,
the teachers, who are "presumed to know." And "as soon as there is
somewhere a subject presumed to know, there is transference" (Lacan
cited in Felman 1987, 85).

But it is *they* who are to listen as we tell our stories. Here lies the
"swerve" in this analogy. The swerve is the surplus, the place of non-
sense, the uncultivated (Serres 1989). The swerve gives us time,

"breathing space" (11) from which to complicate the psychoanalytic analogy. This particular swerve means *sovereignty is not complete*. If it is *they*, our students, who listen, are they not the analysts and we the analysands in this analogy?

Yet such complications are true to the Lacanian psychoanalytic paradigm. Psychoanalysis proceeds, as does teaching, through a kind of "mutual apprenticeship" (Felman 1987, 83). The analyst "attempts to learn from the students his own knowledge" (83). Love, then, is two-way. Lacan insists:

> I deemed it necessary to support the idea of transference, as indistinguishable from love, with the formula of the subject presumed to know.

and

> The question of love is thus linked to the question of knowledge.

and

> Transference *is* love . . . I insist: it is love directed toward, addressed to, knowledge. (All three citations in Felman 1987, 86, emphasis in original)

Or, one could say, listening is love; love pays attention. Thus it occurs only in an open system—that is, an interactive, intertextual system. Kristeva writes, "As implied in modern logical and biological theories dealing with so-called 'open systems,' transference is the Freudian self-organization" (1987, 14). With this, as Felman reminds us,

> the position of the teacher is itself the position of *the one who learns*, of the one who *teaches* nothing other than *the way he learns*. The subject of teaching is interminably—a student; the subject of teaching is interminably—a learning. (1987, 88, emphasis in original)

The articulation of learning/love is also indefinitely deferred.

A coincidence between findings of psychoanalysis and of modern physics (Heisenberg's uncertainty principle) led Lacan to the following pedagogical principle:

> Until further notice, we can say that *the elements do not answer in the place where they are interrogated.* Or more exactly, as soon as they are interrogated somewhere, it is impossible to grasp them in their totality. (cited in Felman 1987, 78, emphasis in original)

This principle is concretely evidenced, for example, by those students who return later to marvel at what they learned in a class and how little they realized it at the time: it is always after the fact, always deferred.

What does it mean to defer love, to defer learning? "Under its sway, one does not speak *of*" (Kristeva 1987, 3, emphasis in original). The rapture of love or learning, as it happens, is unspeakable. Yet, as it happens "one simply has the impression of speaking at last, for the first time, for real" (3). Instances and consequences of deferral are vividly addressed in Toni Morrison's novel *Beloved* (discussed in the next chapter). Such deferral takes different forms and different *distances* (in time/space) from that which "is" or becomes manifest or palpable or articulatable. When that distance becomes too great, as Morrison's characters seem to testify, little good and much harm can come of it. Still, the "right distance" (Taubman 1990) is not clear, nor does Morrison's writing presume to discover that distance as a general principle.

There is another kind of love besides eros, agape, or their synthesis or deconstruction, that is not limited to love between and among human beings. Earlier I flirted with the term *eco-erosic.* That is love of the land (local), and of the earth (global). Love of one's neighbors and intimates (local) and love of humankind (global) cannot be separated from one another or from love of land and earth "under penalty of hatred" (Serres 1992, 20). For if we love one or two exclusively of the others we will do (and have done) great violence in the name of love, "defending" the one against the other. This double law of (eco)love is, for me, the pinnacle of spiritual love and the only law to model in our curricula and in our teaching. Culture is not only about human beings, and it is not only studied as humanities or social sciences. It is also about nature. Science studies *are* cultural studies, claims Donna Harraway (1992). Our construction of "nature" is a co-construction *with* nature. The cultural studies curriculum and classroom is—and this is the bottom line—about this double law of love. And "love in the margins" (Edgerton 1993) is at the base of every good translation.

> These two laws make a single one that combines with both natural and human justice, and which together demand that everyone move from the local to the global, a difficult trail and one not well marked, but one that we must blaze. Never forget the place you come from, but leave it and join the universal. Love the bond that links your earth and the Earth, and that makes the familiar and the foreign, the near and the far, resemble each other. . . . There is nothing real but love, and no law other than this. (Serres 1992, 20–21)

"Hate is the integral of all contraries," says Serres (1982b, 25). Contraries are contradictions, oppositions, opposites. If this is so, love cannot be the opposite of hate as it would then itself be within that integral. A paradox? There is no "solution." The best we can do is attempt to read well, to listen, to set ourselves up for the "surprise of otherness" (Johnson, B. 1987, 15). As such, the "integral of all contraries" is a poor reader. It reads itself into all texts, denying, repressing, and suppressing difference. Denying learning, growth, experience—yet requiring all of those for its very existence and continued dominance. Thus it cannot remain dominant for all situations, for all events, for all time. It moves about and around the margins, where it recuperates by appropriation, by gaining just enough insight to fling itself back to the center to rest and re-atrophy—to re-reify.

Love will resurface. It provides the texture of novels read in chapter four. It appears in the autobiographical writings of myself and some of my students in chapter five. And it is the subjective state within which I have written.

Conclusion

I have argued that a "racialized" standpoint is a marginalized one in addition to a *feminine/feminist* standpoint, and that a feminine/feminist standpoint is more capable of displacing at least three hierarchicalized oppositions (center/margin, mind/body, agape/eros) than is a standpoint at the center. In light of the novels examined in this book, an obvious question is how capable of displacement is a black standpoint relative to the feminist one? I have no intention of attempting to quantify such a comparison in any way. My intent is only to entertain the notion that arguments similar (not identical) to those for a feminist standpoint could be effectively employed for a racialized standpoint.

Expressions of and beliefs about love, indeed about emotion in general, are culturally specific (e.g., see Catherine Lutz's *Unnatural Emotions*, 1988). As such, when I call upon Western Christian concepts as well as Western psychoanalytic concepts of love, limitations must be acknowledged. African-American and African-Caribbean people have, however, "inherited" much that has been called "Western" at the same time European-American and European-Caribbean people have "inherited" (though hugely unacknowledged) much that has been called "African." Still, one of the more emphatic points of this writing is to call attention to, and to explore the ways in which, encounters between cultures are what constitutes the very notion of culture, and that the results of these encounters are manifested in regionally particularistic forms. To the extent that this is so, then, it seems reasonable to look at notions of love through "Western" lenses as long as the lenses are acknowledged and their limitations brought to the surface. It is through readings of literary works that I hope to encounter some of the translations and transformations of these Western notions.

In comparing novels by authors of different racial and gendered positions, a point of interest will be to what extent does the "nonsynchronous" nature of these subjectivities affect their approaches to love and marginality. By nonsynchrony I am referring to a concept of dynamic and contradictory relations of race, class, and gender as theorized by Cameron McCarthy (1988a) whereby, for instance, one's racial interests will, under some circumstances, come into direct conflict with one's gendered interests. Nonsynchrony refers to complex dealings with *differences between*. *Differences within* require an appeal to feminist psychoanalytic, poststructural, and "schizoanalytic" theories. It should be noted that explorations of *difference within* are often relegated to the status of luxury when held next to the necessity of dealing with *difference between* that has been created by historically specific exclusions and oppressions. However, I argue that readings of *differences within* and their interactions with *differences between* are crucial to development of cultural theories that do not disarticulate radical minority and feminist concerns.

Difference is approached in different ways for different historical periods. For the characters of Morrison's *Beloved*, for example, the *difference between* is the difference that most occupies the energies—the *difference between* being social categories of difference that determine historical exclusion and oppression of marginal groups. Still, for these characters to have lives that include love, pleasure, etc., other levels/layers of difference had to come into play. Barbara Johnson's "difference within" is useful but limited for understanding the particular issues at play here. According to Johnson, *differences between* are often illusions created by repression and projection of *differences within*. Both *difference between* and *difference within* can carry negative connotations in the context of my earlier words. That is, either I have an identity foisted upon me from without and I am excluded, or I am repressing parts of myself and thus excluding some ones or some things from my consideration. These connotations belie the positive potential of difference and of marginality. Already I have mentioned the *currere of marginality*, which begins to reveal causes for celebration in difference (without ignoring historically oppressive consequences).

I would like to offer the suggestion that there is another way of thinking about difference that is neither purely *within* nor *between*, and is not based on repression or exclusion in any life-denying senses of those terms, and that is conducive to action in the ethico-aesthetic realms. *Invisible Man*'s invisibility-becoming glimpses at this, I think. The dual or perhaps paradoxical sense of marginality, whereby it serves as both a force that excludes and includes—excludes one from power and yet includes one by promoting forms of knowledge that can be translated into forms of power—seems to parallel Ellison's usages of "leaping outside history." Leaping out in search of a kind of psychic relief from the pressures of invisibility and marginality can be viewed as an act of hopelessness, of abandoning social and political action and retreating into self—an ultimately conservative move much like those of the hysteric and the sorceress as described by Catherine Clement and Helene Cixous (1988). On the other hand, it can be viewed as leaping outside recorded or official history and self-consciously into the more compelling, unwritten history. In this sense it might be thought of as taking the "ultimate" political action of rejecting systems that forbid joy; a way of converting the hysterical laughter into the "god-laugh," ("the god-laugh always seems frivolous" [Robbins 1987, 232]), and searching out and acting out the marginality within.

It seems to me that Ellison is attempting to find a way of taking this leap outside history while continuing to maintain a level of "realism" in which social/political action is more outwardly and materially manifested. That sense of difference, I think, can be theorized through love and learning and through notions such as the three layers of marginality, where individuals are viewed as connected, not harnessed. That sense of difference and identity through cross-cultural imagination and translations of tradition are explored through readings of (and translations across) literary works by Ralph Ellison, Toni Morrison, William Faulkner, Zora Neale Hurston, Mark Twain, and Jamaica Kincaid in the following chapter.

4

Translating Curriculum
with Literature and
Cultural Studies

S TORIES ARE SURVIVAL MATERIAL. They are the means by which we
create and re-create our lives, the medium of the "talking cure,"
and they are tools of our trade as good teachers. There have been
times, and there are still some places, where stories are honored. But,
despite the best efforts of many to restore (re-story?) them to scholarly
legitimacy, stories often do not occupy the status of authority.

In the realm of pedagogy, Felman articulates Lacan's "discipleship"
to Freud *not* in terms of the application of psychoanalysis to pedagogy
but in terms of the *"implication* of psychoanalysis in pedagogy and of
pedagogy in psychoanalysis" (1987, 75, original emphasis). More
precisely,

> what is unique about Freud's position as a student is that he learns
> from, or puts in the position of his teacher, the least authoritative
> sources of information that can be imagined: he knows how to derive
> a teaching, or a lesson, from the very unreliability—the very *nonau-*
> *thority*—of literature, of dreams, or patients. (92, original emphasis)

It is this lesson, according to Felman, that Lacan learns from Freud. The nonauthority of the study of teaching can be read in such a way as well, like (and through) a literary text, or a story. Like the psychoanalytic discipline, the study of teaching produces "a knowledge that does not know what it knows and is thus *not in possession of itself*" (92, original emphasis). Such a knowledge holds certain advantages. It puts us in better stead for exploring the problems of hierarchy, of transference (love), and of translation across difference (translation without a master). I begin the work of this literary chapter by offering a story of my own that links the work of a cultural studies classroom about curriculum and instruction to the realm of literature, story, and history.

The semester before I finished this book I had moved back to Chicago and resumed my position at the University of Illinois. After being away for a year, I found myself faced with the following: a divorce; my previously healthy and lively father suffered a series of strokes and almost died, but came through in need of a wheelchair and constant care for an indefinite amount of time; upon returning from his bedside in Louisiana I became ill and was unable to digest food adequately for a week (that made two weeks of missed classes for the semester); this book was long overdue and under contract; and I fell in love with someone who lives in another city. As one friend put it, I was "taking the advanced course."

Given all the disruption and stress, my teaching was feeling woefully inadequate—like it was possibly the worst it had ever been. I never felt prepared and was always tired and worried. One of my classes was an undergraduate elementary-education methods course in social studies and literature. In past semesters I have struggled with this class, often feeling frustrated by my sense of preservice undergraduate elementary-education student anti-intellectualism.

This time I had a new idea for a class project that was to fulfill all assignment requirements, aside from a weekly journal for brief responses to reading and for comments and questions to me. The project was to take history as central and to build the other social studies and literature studies around it. History was to be the central social studies field for the project because, in my experience, both preservice and practicing elementary teachers tend to feel they lack sufficient background in history, and/or they profess hatred for it due to their own exposure to poor teaching methods around history (i.e., memorizing disconnected dates, "heroes," wars, events, etc.). Students were to choose a particular era, set of events, issues, and/or questions in order to narrow the focus and allow for depth of study. They also had the choice of working alone or in a group.

We started with Howard Zinn's *A People's History of the United States,* reading the first chapter in common so as to understand the rationale for his historical perspective. For the sake of convenience, students chose a chapter from that book to begin their individual projects—a chapter that dealt with a topic they wanted personally to know more about. I took on Columbus's encounters with indigenous peoples in the "New World" as my own project because that came from the Zinn chapter we had read in common. The projects were done in three phases, each one a revision and extension of the last. For each phase, I presented my own work a week before theirs was due so that I could ease them into a place of greater confidence about expectations and possibilities. Doing a project myself better enabled me to empathize with their difficulties . . . plus I was learning a great deal about something I was interested in. From there the project went in a number of directions.

We read a variety of adult-level renderings of our chosen stories. We found stories from other social studies disciplines that were in some way related (e.g., for mine there were map studies from the 15th century, economics behind Columbian exploits, and cultural contexts at that time in Europe and the Caribbean). We examined several elementary-education social studies textbook renderings of the "same story" and compared that to what we were learning. We looked at fiction, poetry, film, and art surrounding that story. We found children's literature, old and new, that related to, or helped to tell that story. Finally, we worked to come up with a variety of meaningful ways to share what we were learning with children.

I could see from the early presentations that some good work was being produced. Students had chosen the Vietnam War, women's rights, slavery, civil rights, the Civil War, World War II, labor movements and the Great Depression, and Native American history. And in almost every case students were adopting Zinn's perspective, for at least part of the time, by looking at history from the standpoint of those who lost the most rather than gained the most. Nonetheless, students *seemed* in class to be bored, restless, typically unengaged as any students I'd ever had for this course. This time I really thought it was my fault due to my personal difficulties. Hence, I expected little.

The profundity of what was happening in that class finally began to dawn on me near the end, when one student came to my office and offered testimony. She said the project was the most meaningful endeavor (both personally and professionally) she had undertaken in the college of education, that she would keep it for the rest of her life, that she sent it to an incarcerated cousin who became excited about it and wanted more, and that she would continue to work on it. I cried, but supposed she was a unique case.

Then, in the last two weeks, when everyone displayed and talked about her or his project before turning it in, there came a great flood of testimony. Several students spoke enthusiastically and at length about how much they had learned, when they could have opted to end the last two classes quickly by rushing through their presentations. Most said that they would *never* again rely on textbooks alone (either for themselves or their students). Many said that although they hated history before, they were interested now. Many said they now understood that this kind of work is important to good teaching, and felt more confident about their ability to do it. Several said they would keep and continue to work on the project, that they now understood what it means to feel passion about learning, and that they even had fun doing this. Again, I was overwhelmed. It felt real. (Students in this big-city school are not in the habit of flattering professors!)

There are several reasons I chose to tell this story as the preface to a chapter on literature, cultural studies, and curriculum. First, like many others I've spoken to, I've found teaching classes about cultural diversity in separate multicultural education courses is often extremely frustrating for a number of reasons. Most frustrating is the resentment and resistance so many students exhibit toward the course material. However, in this methods class many of the goals of my multicultural classes were met, but without didacticism about culture and politics that is so difficult to avoid in separate courses. *And this happened with a cultural studies approach.* Students found out for themselves about the connections of culture and politics today to our histories and to the institution of schooling. They learned about the marketing strategies of textbook publishers firsthand, and what that meant for the schooling of children and themselves on many levels. Through their own projects, and those of their classmates, they were able to see the connections between past and present, history and economics and other disciplines, one place and another. I did not have to tell them. Furthermore, they gained competence and confidence for doing deep scholarly work, and found the pleasure in it as well as its relevance for teaching young children. I did not have to ask them to take my word about the value in this.

Second, this chapter is about stories, reading, and interpretation, and their relation to teaching. This is a story about my own reading of a teaching situation—a very good reading on an unconscious or a subconscious level (a literacy of the imagination?), and a very poor reading on a more conscious level (a blocked, neurotic reading?). This experience demonstrated for me something like my *knowledge that did not know what it knows.*

Third, literature as a teaching tool became clearly vital to *every* project in this elementary-education social studies class. The students drew on written histories, various social studies texts, and even film. But they also discovered the vitality and centrality of literature to their own engagement, and for filling in the gaps left by textbooks. Some even wrote poetry and/or used poetry by others. For the first time in my teaching career I felt students in my class gained a deep appreciation for the *truths* that are embodied in the arts—truths that fill in the gaps left by "official knowledge." Literature and poetry became absolutely necessary to them.

This chapter is also about how the literary works I read and interpret have taught me about teaching. I've not only learned history, narrative style and function, literary criticism, cultural studies, and philosophy from such reading, I've also *learned about learning,* about loving, and about listening. It is obvious now to me that this informs my teaching in major ways—ways that came through in that traumatic semester without my even knowing it. Literature is not the only way to do this work, but it certainly is one very good way, and a way that compels me.

Love and learning—the pedagogical imperative within each novel examined below—are two organizing themes for my approach to reading. Indeed, as I have implied before, neither literacy of the imagination nor cross-cultural literacy is possible outside these themes. Where appropriate, the pedagogical relations between the texts are also highlighted. The search for *voice* impels much of the "literature of the margins"[1] to proceed through a pedagogical imperative. In Twain and Faulkner, for example, *voice* is not sought for key characters to the same extent that it is in the novels by Hurston, Morrison, Ellison, and Kincaid. The journey for Huck and Jim is at times, and in ways, one of love and learning (learning to love). But Huck's search for *voice* is repeatedly frustrated (blocked), and Jim's is unpursued or unexamined. The same frustration is found in *Absalom, Absalom!* Major characters remain obsessed until death. In both novels the limits of *voice* seem somewhat prefigured. That is, *voice* is taken for granted and thus not sought, not expanded. *Voice*, such as it is here, functions through a block that obsesses on the same story and reads it into every other story.

Learning to "read the world" is inseparable from learning to read, to speak, to create one's "self." Literacy and *voice* are not properly separable if we mean by literacy something beyond the "garden variety" block-function literacy whereby we read competently only in a singular way. Our reading of literary works is facilitated by a *literacy of the imagination* even as we encounter characters (and sometimes authors) who read the world only, or sometimes, in blocks. We might locate dominant narratives, or blocks, in our reading by taking explicit aim at the margins that emerge and the ways in which these literary works translate between and among one another and/or between and among tradition(s) (e.g., canonical works or works that express the block functions as well as the meaningful myth and ritual of entire cultures). How are margins and centers articulated? In exploring the novels' responses to that question, essentializing movements and gestures are uncovered as well as the ways these movements and gestures negotiate with identity formation or the search for voice. In the translations between novels that take place, block functions, margins, centers, *histories* are rewritten, rearticulated.

I write from the assumption that the novels are familiar to the reader as they are mostly well-known works. If and when a literary work here is unfamiliar, I invite the reader to imagine the stories, suspending disbelief until (and if desired) the novel can be read.

Intertextual Literary Readings

Invisible Man is the story of an African American man who, like author Ralph Ellison, grew up and went to school in the South, then moved north in the 1930s. It is also the story of a black man struggling to create and sustain a livable identity for himself through the absurdity and violence of unrelenting white racism. The journey transpires through a series of associations, frustrations, and blocks, each passage giving rise to new ways of reading for *Invisible Man* and the reader of this novel.

Love as an explicit thought comes late in Ralph Ellison's *Invisible Man*, though its expression is implicit throughout. It seems that Invisible Man approaches and touches the power of his own displaced (interactive) marginality repeatedly but always heads back for his (nondisplaced) center. While at first read female players seem notably marginal in the text, closer readings reveal them as more significant and mutually marginalized players. They seem to lead him into consciousness of his own marginalization and victimization (invisibility). They are, according to Claudia Tate,

> like the underground station masters of the American slave era [assisting him] along his course to freedom. . . . They embody the knowledge he needs to state his escape. (Tate 1987, 164–65)

Tate speculates in her essay "Notes on the Invisible Women in Ralph Ellison's *Invisible Man*," that the women in this novel are crucial to each major turning point in Invisible Man's growing self and social awareness. The nude "magnificent blonde" at the battle royal "provides . . . his first lesson in invisibility" (167) as he recognizes their mutual objectification/exploitation and her "Kewpie Doll mask" response to it (167). The second major breakthrough occurs, according to Tate, after Mary Rambo emotionally and physically nurtures him back to a state of greater self-esteem, such that he can "depart from the world of 'Keep This Nigger-Boy Running'" at least for a while (168). His third and fourth lessons come from the women of the Brotherhood. He is able to overcome the anxiety of confronting the taboo around sexual encounters between black men and white women with Emma and the anonymous rich white woman, as well as to identify somewhat with their common exploitation. Finally, with Sybil he comes not only to recognize invisibility but also to appreciate the potential power in it.

> But before he can clearly see his relationship with the magnificent blonde, Emma, and the anonymous seductress and acknowledge their respective marginality, alienation, and ultimately their respective invisibility, he must dance his third and final dance, in which his partner is Sybil. . . . Sybil, like Mary, is another surrogate mother who comes to deliver the young protagonist from the deception of his false identity with the Brotherhood. She is also another symbolic blonde, who ushers him to the threshold of the final battle royal. In addition, she is his last teacher, who propels him along the course to freedom by making him aware that invisibility is not necessarily a liability but possibly a valuable asset. (169–70)

And it is this recognition of mutual marginalization that finally brings Invisible Man to an appreciation for the necessity of love to life and to action—love, but not to the exclusion of justifiable and motivating anger; love, but not self-obliterating or self-submerging love.

> So why do I write, torturing myself to put it down? Because in spite of myself I've learned some things. Without the possibility of action, all knowledge comes to one labeled "file and forget," and I can neither file nor forget. Nor will certain ideas forget me; they keep filing away at my lethargy, my complacency. . . . I denounce because though implicated and partially responsible, I have been hurt to the point of abysmal pain, hurt to the point of invisibility. And I defend

because in spite of all I find that I love. In order to get some of it down I *have* to love. (Ellison 1952, 566–67, emphasis in original)

When Ellison writes of love at this time, I do not feel that he means it only in terms of agape or "brotherly love." Indeed, it was his encounter with Sybil which was simultaneously sexually, emotionally, and intellectually moving for him that seemed to trigger thoughts of love and the connections between love and social action. Further, he displaces the "masculine" hierarchy of thinking/feeling in the following passage:

There is, by the way, an area in which a man's feelings are more rational than his mind, and it is precisely in that area that his will is pulled in several directions at the same time. (560)

Listening is love. Or at least that might be what Kristeva is saying when she calls transference love "optimum"—optimum because it "avoids the chaotic hyperconnectedness of fusion love as well as the death-dealing stabilization of love's absence" (1987, 15). Sybil listened. It was an agapic listening without judgement, an erosic listening with her body, and there was exchange of those between them. Invisible Man seemed to be shocked into awareness that this mass of human beings outside consisted of many individuals who love and listen and are loved and listened to.

Listening, like engagement with a text, effects a dissolution of the boundaries of self. So does love. Simultaneously frightening and exhilarating, it allows the "outside" to come "inside," opening up channels of possibility, sharing languages, inspiring action. Love conceived in this way could become part of what Guattari calls a "mental ecology"—that is, an ecology that can

face up to the logic of the ambivalence of desire [eros], . . . re-evaluate the ultimate goal of work and human activities in terms of criteria other than those of profit and productivity [relationality], acknowledge the need to mobilize individuals and social segments in ways that are always diverse and different. (1990, 9)

It is schizophrenic—"his will is pulled in several directions at the same time" (Ellison 1952, 560)—leaping into difference and otherness. But this schizophrenia can become a "positive schizophrenic line of escape" (Deleuze and Guattari 1983, 363), or it can become "neuroticized" (363) as narcissistic "fusion love" (pure eros) and from other manifestations of codes relinquished to institutions (Kristeva 1987). I should add that in Kristeva's terms, as for Lacan, narcissism is not simply flawed. It is a necessary condition of human love and life.

> What stands between the subject and his desire for death is narcissism. The relationship between narcissism and aggressiveness makes for the fact that narcissism, the ecstatic affirmation of one's being alive, is always enacted at someone's expense. The affirmation of one's life entails the exploitation of someone else's life. (Schneiderman 1980, 6)

Whereas the risk in translation or pursuit of knowledge is the risk of violence, the pursuit of love, teaching, the work that strives to minimize violence, is interminable, impossible, and vital.

"Fusion love" is excessive in its narcissism—"its Highness the Ego projects and glorifies itself, or else shatters into pieces and is engulfed" (Schneiderman 1980, 6). This is eros, untempered by agape. Fusion is what, in Toni Morrison's *Beloved*, Sethe's love for Beloved (the ghost) became for a time (more on this later). But I do not believe it started that way with Beloved (the child). Love can be murderous as a result of fusion, but love—especially perhaps mother-love—complicated by the ravages of the almost total social marginalization that is slavery, can be cataclysmic. Killing the child to save her from slavery might have been, as Morrison said, "the right thing to do [but] she had no right to do it" (Otten 1989, 83).

Paul D is suspicious and frightened of loving too big or too much. Sethe's love seems often all-consuming and without boundaries. Paul D first becomes aware of and is alarmed by Sethe's seemingly boundless mother-love when she attempts to apologize for Denver's (Sethe's daughter named after the poor white girl, Amy Denver, who helped Sethe) rudeness to Paul D, and then to disallow him to confront

Denver directly about it. He feels that it is "very risky. For a used-to-be-slave woman to love anything that much" given the fate of so many relationships under slavery. One must "love . . . everything, just a little bit [so that] maybe you'd have a little love left over for the next one" (Morrison 1987, 45). Later, upon discovering that Sethe had murdered her baby girl, Paul D is horrified and uncomprehending of the source, meaning, and implications of such love.

> This here Sethe talked about love like any other woman, . . . but what she meant could cleave the bone. This here Sethe talked about safety with a handsaw. This here new Sethe didn't know where the world stopped and she began. . . . More important than what Sethe had done was what she claimed. It scared him.
>
>   "Your love is too thick". . . "You got two feet, Sethe, not four," he said, and right then a forest sprang up between them; trackless and quiet. (164–65)

The murderous spectacle put on for the white inquisitors (the masters from whom Sethe ran away) was indeed sufficient to save herself and other children from returning to slavery. Spectacular expressions such as the woman who responded to her first bidder at the slave auction by chopping off her own hand with a hatchet were not so uncommon to slave women (Fox-Genovese 1988, 329). Finally, she is heard. But the incident was permanently inscribed in the memory of herself, her sons and the community as a horrifying reminder of the tenuousness of their integrity as a community, as loving individuals, as families. She "buried" the memory with the child, purchasing a headstone with yet another indignity—selling her body to another white exploiter.

With the unexpected arrival of Paul D, the task for Sethe and he and Denver becomes that of dealing somehow with this repressed past that interferes with their abilities to feel for themselves and one another. Paul D had always "dealt" with his own past by moving around, effectively denying it. But now he wanted to stop and settle with the person who had known him longer than anyone else.

The ghost (proper) of Beloved, who had earlier been maintaining Sethe and Denver without serious challenges, had now been run off by Paul D. Sethe, Denver, or both had to bring her back in a form that could not be denied by Paul D. Beloved's (re)appearance at a crucial point in the development of the (love) relationship between Sethe and Paul D has the effect of stopping the painful process of love/analysis (pedagogy). Paul D and Sethe had been serving as one another's "analysts" (teachers), but a new analyst had to enter the picture for the cure to be effected.

The analysis proceeds pathologically. Paul D participates in exhuming this past by impregnating the ghost, the analyst, Sethe's past. This act could be seen as a response to fear of love—fear, indeed, of the object of Sethe's love, knowing what her love can lead to. On the other hand he provided her past, her ghost, with possibilities (pregnant with possibilities), but in doing so it almost consumes Sethe. With Beloved as analyst, Sethe's transference love quickly escalates out of control. As the boundaries between Sethe and the one she loves obsessively (Beloved) are further diminished by this love of hers, her "self" declines mentally and physically to a dangerously marginal place. Boundaries dissolve to the point that Sethe's love must be a kind of self-love/self-hate, excessively narcissistic.

But what is Denver's stake in all this? She is fascinated with the ghost (Sethe made?). Why? Sethe, the one Denver loves, is afraid of her own love, understandably, and that fear/love takes the form of the ghost. Denver is fascinated with the "abject"—the object of her mother's fear and love. Kristeva writes that the abject is at the margins of life/death, "the edge of non-existence," and is signified by waste, corpses (ghosts?) (1982, 1–11).

Meanwhile, Paul D is plowing through an emotional crisis of his own. It is when their respective crises of love reach a climax (the analysis is complete when the pregnancy "ends") that both Paul D and Sethe together find a place for love that could be characterized as displacement of the agape/eros, or of the (fear and distance)/(self-obliterating love), hierarchy. Much of this work is done via Stamp Paid and Denver through the legacy of love left behind by Baby Suggs, who had arrived upon a "deconstruction" of those dualisms long ago. Suggs preached love of body, love of self and, in the "same breath," Christian love (Morrison 1987, 88–89).

While in *Beloved*'s conclusion the possibility for love not based on opposition seems imminent, the fate of Invisible Man is less clear. He has become aware of his invisibility/marginality and what that can do for him. But his notion of love is still quite vague and undeveloped, and he has yet to sustain an intimate relationship in the context of this new self-awareness.

Recognition of marginality and allusions to its paradoxical nature and its "usefulness" are sprinkled throughout the experience of Invisible Man. Invisibility can be used synonymously with marginality at the social level in the sense that it means invisible to "others." At the individual level invisibility is synonymous with marginality in the sense of its being self-awareness that is most difficult to come by—it is hidden from the self. Invisible Man begins his journey blind to his own invisibility but by the end of this text he insists that he is "invisible, not blind" (Ellison 1952, 563).

In the beginning he is unable to draw on the power that his marginality can provide. He is baffled and plagued by his Grandfather's dying words about what it means to "yes them to death," and he participates in his own exploitation and display in order to attend a school where he is "named . . . and set running with one and the same stroke of the pen" (555). This pattern continues far beyond the point at which he has caught the first glimpses of his invisibility, on into his work for the Brotherhood where he thought he could lead an "historically meaningful life." It seems significant that the most explicit and clearly articulated verbal lessons he is given about invisibility are from a "fat man" (also black) who was committed to an insane asylum and was formerly a physician—one who seems to embody "order out of chaos" (or vice versa). Speaking of Invisible Man:

> Already he's learned to repress not only his emotions but his humanity. He's invisible, a walking personification of the Negative, the most perfect achievement of your dreams sir! The mechanical man! (92)

And then later, on the train to New York:

You're hidden right out in the open—that is, you would be if you only realized it. They wouldn't see you because they don't expect you to know anything, since they believe they've taken care of that. . . . (152)

To merely hear it verbalized was not enough because it did not yet name his experience sufficiently. Invisible Man had to experience more. If naming experience is the first step to forming a sense of autonomy, then "claiming ownership of that freed self" (Morrison 1987, 95) is one step beyond that. Upon finally realizing the true agenda of the Brotherhood, Invisible Man is flooded with the realizations that

They had set themselves up to describe the world. . . . It was as though I'd learned suddenly to look around corners; images of past humiliations flickered through my head and I saw that they were more than separate experiences. They were me; they defined me. I was my experiences and my experiences were me, and no blind men, no matter how powerful they became, . . . could take that. . . . Here I had thought they accepted me because they felt that color made no difference, when in reality it made no difference because they didn't see either color or men . . . I now recognized my invisibility. (Ellison 1952, 496–97)

This is the point at which Sybil becomes instrumental in Invisible Man's "loss of illusions." Allusions throughout the book to loss of eyes, a glass eye, blindness, and castration begin to coalesce into a network of symbolism. Houston Baker claims that black male sexuality is a key theme of the novel and that it is rarely dealt with by literary critics (329). Trueblood as object of fascination for whites, merges with Norton's phrase "casting out the offending eye," the imagery of blindness and illusion, the threat of castration at the factory hospital, and finally Invisible Man's dream of having been castrated by Jack—his testicles at times described more like eyes. Confronting the repression of black male sexuality with regard to white women becomes a crucial interconnected symbolic expression of freedom, marginality, and love. White woman represents

the means by which black people in general were penalized for exer-
cising the freedom of choice, in that the penalty was translated into
the accusation of rape and the sentence was death. The symbolic linkage between the white woman and freedom, therefore, finds its origin
in hundreds of years of southern race relations. (Tate 1987, 166)

Returning to his grandfather's dying advice, Invisible Man asks the
question again, what did he mean by saying "yes"? As he explores the
possibilities, more capable of imagination now, he stumbles upon a *currere of marginality:*

> Was it that we of all, we, most of all, had to affirm the principle [upon
> which the country was built], the plan in whose name we had been
> brutalized and sacrificed—not because we would always be weak nor
> because we were afraid or opportunistic, but because we were older
> than they, in the sense of what it took to live in the world with others
> and because they had exhausted in us, some—not much, but some—
> of the human greed and smallness, yes, and the fear and superstition
> that had kept them running. (Oh, yes, they're running too, running
> all over themselves.) (Ellison 1952, 561)

And he further captures the notion of the paradox of marginality both
in a Freirian dialectical sense and in the sense of Spivak's deconstructivist thought:

> Weren't we part of them as well as apart from them and subject to die
> when they died? . . . It's "winner take nothing" that is the great truth
> of our country or of any country. Life is to be lived, not controlled;
> and humanity is won by continuing to play in face of certain defeat.
> Our fate is to become one, and yet many—This is not prophecy, but
> description. (1988, 562, 564)

Like Ellison, Morrison uncovers a paradoxical *currere of marginality*
in *Beloved.* The carnival, which allowed for a "Colored Thursday," was
a chance unbeknownst to the white carnival-folk for black people to
"see the spectacle of whitefolks making a spectacle of themselves"

(1987, 48). Another example of black "Signifyin(g)" on whites is Paul D's "chain-gang":

> With a sledge hammer in his hands and Hi Man's lead, the men got through. They sang it out and beat it up, garbling the words so they could not be understood; tricking the words so their syllables yielded up other meanings. . . . They killed a boss so often and so completely they had to bring him back to life to pulp him one more time. (108, 109)

The power of marginality in the external world is dampened in *Beloved* compared to *Invisible Man*, due to the difference in the larger social situation of the time settings. Nor is it a given—it is problematic and paradoxical. The "meanness" of the black community toward Sethe resonates with Invisible Man's recognition that only "some—not much, but some—of the human greed and smallness, . . . and the fear and superstition" had been exhausted in blacks relative to whites (Ellison 1952, 561).

Boundaries between social categories that are represented as natural ones are exposed as fraudulent in *Beloved* as they are in *Invisible Man* ("a part as well as apart"). This displacement also arises in the blurring of self/other for black/white, but Morrison approaches it from a different perspective than that of Ellison—namely, she sees black in white whereas Ellison sees white in black.

> Whitepeople believed that whatever the manners, under every dark skin was a jungle. Swift unnavigable waters, swinging screaming baboons, sleeping snakes, red gums ready for their sweet white blood. In a way, he thought, they were right. The more coloredpeople spent their strength trying to convince them how gentle they were, how clever and loving, how human, the more they used themselves up to persuade whites of something Negroes believed could not be questioned, the deeper and more tangled the jungle grew inside. But it wasn't the jungle blacks brought with them to this place from the other (livable) place. It was the jungle whitefolks planted in them. . . . It spread. . . . it spread, until it invaded the whites who had made it. . . . The screaming baboon lived under their own white skin; the red gums were their own. (Morrison 1987, 198–99)

Ultimately, for Sethe it is the love she negotiates with Paul D that allows her the awareness that she is indeed her own "best thing." Like Invisible Man this negotiated, "deconstructed" love provides the turning-around place for a more autonomous, yet connected, life. The difference between the two novels with regard to love that is most pronounced is the different directions from which the deconstruction was approached. For Morrison, Sethe had come from an almost complete reversal of the agape/eros hierarchy in her mother-love for first Denver, then Beloved (as ghost). For Ellison, Invisible Man seemed to begin with very little self-definition for the concept of love. But in those situations, dominant oppositions tend to win by default. These different starting places affected approaches to other oppositions as well. Blurred boundaries in *Beloved* became more distinct, clear distinctions became more fluid in *Invisible Man*—more fluid in spite of his wary tendency to keep things divided.

Love and the pedagogical imperative that lives in these novels are not bounded by the confines of expressions among characters only within their respective texts. That is, Sethe "speaks" beyond the pages of *Beloved* and Invisible Man beyond the pages of *Invisible Man*. For example, both have been read as, in part, rereadings and rewritings of Mark Twain's *Adventures of Huckleberry Finn* (Moreland 1991; Nadel 1988). In *Beloved*, Sethe, a pregnant woman who had just suffered a severe beating by her master, runs away from slavery by crossing the Ohio River from Kentucky into Ohio. But before she makes it across, exhausted, hungry and about to deliver, she collapses, where she might have died had not a young poor white runaway girl, Amy Denver, happened upon her, taken care of her, and helped to deliver the child. As Richard Moreland notes, there are parallels with the relationship between Sethe and Amy and the one between Huck and Jim, a difference being it is Sethe's journey (Jim's counterpart), not Amy's (Huck's counterpart), that is of primary concern in Morrison's story. Furthermore, Sethe and others find a voice in Morrison's story. Neither Huck nor Jim are ever able to fully articulate their positions in Twain's story.

Ellison's *Invisible Man*, on the other hand, represents an effort to continue the search for a voice not only for Jim, who might seem the logical counterpart to Invisible Man as both are black, but also for Huck. Nadel sees Invisible Man as vacillating between Jim and Huck.

> The point is that at various stages throughout the book, the Invisible Man plays Huck and at others Jim, as often subconsciously as consciously.
>
> The problem for Ellison at the time he was writing *Invisible Man* was that we didn't have a literature which permitted those roles for blacks. (1988, 143)

"For Ellison," according to Nadel, "Twain was the last great American author to see the full implications of the connection between the black and the fundamentals of democracy" (127). In this spirit, in 1947 Ellison rereads and rewrites Twain's story of Huck and Jim amidst a sea of unfavorable criticism for Twain's book, particularly its last section.

This sort of retelling can be thought of as an example of what Gates calls "Signifyin'"—a tradition in Black English vernacular. Zora Neale Hurston was possibly the first to theorize about black "Signifying" through her studies as an anthropologist on African-American and African-Caribbean culture, particularly through folk storytelling. It is a major tropological strategy employed in her novel *Their Eyes Were Watching God.* This trope is a focus for Gates. He calls it the trope of the "Signifyin(g) Monkey." The "g" in Signifyin(g) is a "Signifyin(g) upon" Derrida's "misspelling" of the French difference to differance, which Gates does, as does Derrida, in order to retain an instability for meaning of the term. Signifyin(g) is a repetition and a reversal (chiasmus) of a sentence, phrase, or idea, and has been a part of African-American vernacular tradition since antebellum America—even referred to in common conversation as "signifyin upon" (1987).

In order to more clearly explicate this concept I'll pull out some examples provided by Gates. Jazz music often proceeds through "signifying riffs." For example, when John Coltrane performs *My Favorite Things* he is Signifyin(g) upon Julie Andrews "vapid original." It is "repetition of a form and inversion of the same.... Resemblance ... evoked cleverly by dissemblance" (1987, 243). And, as an example in language, Gates provides the following anecdote:

> While writing this essay, I asked a colleague, Dwight Andrews, if he had heard of the Signifying Monkey as a child. "Why, no" he replied intently. "I never heard of the Signifying Monkey until I came to Yale and read about him in a book." I had been signified upon. If I had responded to Andrews, "I know what you mean; your Mama read to me from that same book the last time I was in Detroit," I would have signified upon him in return. (1987, 293)

Signifyin(g) "constitutes an implicit parody of a subject's own complicity in illusion" (240). It has no equal in "standard English" usage. It is at a level of sophistication in common usage unique, in North America and the Caribbean, to "Black English." A key aspect of Signifyin(g) is its "indirect intent":

> The apparent significance of the message differs from its real significance. The apparent meaning of the sentence signifies its actual meaning. (Mitchell-Kernan 1973, 325)

Signifyin(g) can take the form of irony, parody, or pastiche, and thus as a language form is not the exclusive province of black people; but black people named the term, invented the unique rituals associated with it, and self-consciously use both the strategy and the term itself in everyday conversation (Gates 1988, 90). Parody is the form taken by what Gates calls "motivated Signifyin(g)" and involves negative critique or polemic. Pastiche corresponds to "unmotivated Signifyin(g)," which is not to imply a lack of intention but more a lack of negative critique. As examples of each, Gates calls upon Ishmael Reed's *Mumbo Jumbo* for "motivated Signifyin(g)" on Richard Wright's *Native Son* and Ralph Ellison's *Invisible Man,* and Alice Walker's *The Color Purple* as "unmotivated Signifyin(g)" on Zora Neale Hurston's *Their Eyes Were Watching God.* Gates explains the difference as follows:

> Whereas Reed seems to be about the clearing of a space of narration, Walker seems to be intent on underscoring the relation of her text to Hurston's, in a joyous proclamation of antecedent and descendant texts. . . . This form of the double-voiced implies unity and resemblance rather than critique and difference. (1988, xxvii)

In *Invisible Man* Ellison not only retells Twain's story, he also, according to Nadel, alludes to literary criticism of *Adventures of Huckleberry Finn* that was written by Leslie Fiedler (Nadel 1988), where he signifies on Fiedler in the sense of parody—albeit a loving parody. Briefly, what Fiedler had suggested was that the relationship between Huck and Jim was a homoerotic one which, according to Fiedler is the only possible response to feelings of love between black and white men in America.

> So buried at a level of acceptance which does not touch reason, so desperately repressed from overt recognition, so contrary to what is usually thought of as our ultimate level of taboo—the sense of that love can survive only in the obliquity of a symbol, persistent, obsessive, in short, an archetype. (cited in Nadel 1988, 127)

In *Invisible Man* young Emerson (another allusion) is the homosexual son of a man to whom Invisible Man was sent to find a job. Invisible Man enters this place of business with an unopened letter of "recommendation" in hand that turns out to be a slanderous letter of nonrecommendation. Finally, it is young Emerson who reveals to Invisible Man what has happened. But he does so under the condition that Invisible Man not tell Emerson's father what he has done, leaving Invisible Man helpless to defend himself. In telling Invisible Man his own story, Emerson refers to himself as "Huckleberry" and invites him to a gay black and white nightclub.

The purpose behind Ellison's subtext response to Fiedler in *Invisible Man*, Nadel suggests, is to demonstrate the consequences of Fiedler's reading of Twain and implicitly of American society. If Fiedler is correct, then "Huckish" attempts to help black people out of untenable situations that result from racism are meaningless—only Huck's guilty conscience is real, and his act of freeing Jim amounts to nothing. As Nadel explains:

> Huck does not feel guilt about Jim's enslavement nearly so much as he does about his desire to end that enslavement, and Huck's act of personal responsibility is defined by what he does in spite of his guilt,

not because of it. . . . Fiedler, on the other hand, does not see in Huck's story that his action defies his guilt so much as that his guilt substitutes for action. (1988, 129)

I have called Ellison's parody loving though "motivated" because it retains a sense of the plausibility of Fiedler's conclusions for particular people, places, and times. In fact, Ellison wrote directly to Fiedler's criticism ten years later in which he explains how Twain's depiction of Jim understandably produces misreadings by black critics.

> Twain fitted Jim into the outlines of the minstrel tradition, and it is from behind this stereotype mask that we see Jim's dignity and human capacity—and Twain's complexity—emerge. (cited in Nadel 1988, 130)

And by depicting Huck "with his street-sparrow sophistication," (cited in Nadel, 130) Ellison adds, Huck seems more adult than Jim. Because of this affront, it is understandable that a black reader would be upset. Of Fiedler's reading Ellison says,

> I believe him so profoundly disturbed by the manner in which the deep dichotomies symbolized by blackness and whiteness are resolved that, forgetting to look at the specific form of the novel, he leaped squarely into the middle of that tangle of symbolism which he is dedicated to unsnarling, and yelled out his most terrifying name for chaos. (cited in Nadel, 131)

Through much of the text of *Invisible Man* Twain's text is commented upon directly in what more closely resembles "unmotivated Signifyin(g)." Nadel refers to this rereading and rewriting as allusion and "translating tradition" rather than "Signifyin(g)," but I want to insist on the similarity between the two. Just as with parody and pastiche, allusion is not the sole province of black literary practice. However, the idea of Signifyin' which goes by that name is explicitly named and practiced within African-American vernacular tradition, whereas parody, pastiche, irony, and allusion are literary modes or tropes common to perhaps all literary traditions. Allusion as Nadel discusses it in his theoretical text is not directed only at a black literary tradition but is intended for more general application.

Signifyin' has been useful for thinking about black literary theory in that it can signal very specific modes of parody or pastiche, such as those that focus on black vernacular language usage and Black English usage in particular. Gates and others insist such culturally specific theoretical categories are important to reveal and to apply to culturally specific literature, such as African, African-American, or African-Caribbean, in order to avoid what Anthony Appiah calls "the Naipaul fallacy" (cited in Gates 1986, 405). This fallacy refers to attempts to establish the worthiness of, say, African literature by holding it up to European literature in order to show that they are the same. It can likewise involve attempts to "understand Africa by embedding it in European culture," for example (405).

Nadel traces the Signifyin(g) or alluding parallels between Ellison's and Twain's texts intricately. A detailed reproduction of his reading does not serve my purposes at this point. Following, however, are highlights of his reading: Nadel compares the paint factory incident where Invisible Man is tricked into having a serious accident (at the factory where young Emerson sent him to work) with the destruction of the raft in *Adventures of Huckleberry Finn* by the riverboat; members of the Brotherhood are referred to by Nadel as "latter-day Tom Sawyers" in their betrayals of Invisible Man; Invisible Man is, at times, compared to Jim as being one who is also invisible, and at times, to Huck in his journeying to find a place where he wouldn't have to be ashamed.

The last third of Twain's book has been the most controversial. It has been variously regarded as bad writing, a mistake, or misplaced. Ernest Hemingway wrote, "If you read it you must stop where the Nigger Jim is stolen from the boys. That is the real end. The rest is just cheating" (cited in Nadel 1988, 22). Contrary to this opinion Ellison writes, "Huck Finn's acceptance of the evil implicit in his 'emancipation' of Jim represents Twain's acceptance of his personal responsibility in the condition of society. This was the tragic face behind his comic mask" (Ellison 1953, 50).

Ellison rewrites this part of Twain's text through Invisible Man's encounters with the Brotherhood, a group of mostly male, mostly white orthodox Marxist activists. Invisible Man was selected by the Brotherhood to be their "mouthpiece" for the people of Harlem. However, when Invisible Man delivers a particularly moving speech that speaks to the hearts of Harlem residents, the Brotherhood becomes upset. They now insist on training Invisible Man in the *correct* "scientific" way to work for them—to give speeches. This as opposed to his

> appeal to the heart, the emotions of his audience. . . . This reversal and subsequent effects of his training on his humanity create a discomfort similar to the one created when Tom decides to show Huck the "proper" way to free Jim. (Nadel 1988, 137)

This alludes to Tom Sawyer's rules for his and Huck's plan of escape for Jim. Rather than simply releasing Jim from the prison-hut where he is chained in the easiest, quickest, most obvious manner, Tom insists,

> It don't make no difference how foolish it is, it's the right way—and it's the regular way. And there ain't no *other* way, that ever *I* heard of; and I've read all the books that gives any information about these things. (Twain 1985, 304, emphasis in original)

The Brotherhood represents those (literary) theorists who "define history and exclude from it those who don't confirm their theories" (Nadel 1988, 137). Jim's treatment at the hands of Tom parallels the Brotherhood's treatment of Invisible Man in many ways. Tom (the Brotherhood) sabotage Jim (Invisible Man) in their quests for freedom (black empowerment). A reversal in this repetition is that Invisible Man is Huck as much as he is Jim. It is Huck, as well as Jim, who is being manipulated by Tom. Huck's complicity in his own manipulation also resembles that of Invisible Man's involvement with the Brotherhood. In doing this Ellison directs us toward the last part of *Adventures of Huckleberry Finn*—the part that is Twain's "way of showing the seriousness of Huck's and Jim's dilemma, the full implications of recognizing Jim's humanity" (138).

Ellison reveals the frustration of hopes for freedom and democracy in this part of Twain's novel through his allusions to it and Signifyin(g) upon it in *Invisible Man*. Moreland suggests, "it is this frustration that I think Morrison brilliantly addresses in *Beloved*" (1991, 2). As such, insofar as Morrison's text is Signifyin(g) upon Twain's, it too seems to fit more closely Gates's notion of an "unmotivated Signifyin(g)."

Moreland reads Morrison's "put[ting] his [Twain's] story next to hers" (2), in part, through the "ecosophy" of Guattari, whose notions of de-territorialization and reterritorialization I have related to my use of translation in chapter three (1990). For Guattari, the beginning of this process is marked by "a-signifying ruptures," which Moreland sees as represented by the frustration repeatedly provoked in generations of *Adventures of Huckleberry Finn* readers—frustrations born of the persistent resistance of Twain's novel to providing satisfactory resolutions. Language and style that were needed to express such resolutions were not available to Twain until Morrison's text entered it. Moreland cites Guattari:

> At the heart of all ecological praxes is an a-signifying rupture in a context in which the catalysts of existential change are present, but lack expressive support from the enunciative assemblage which frames them. (8)

And further,

> In the absence of ecological praxis, those catalysts remain inactive and tend towards inconsistency; they produce anxiety, guilt, other forms of psychopathological repetition. (8)

Moreland adds, "by putting Twain's novel next to Morrison's, anticipating Morrison's" (8) one finds an example of Guattari's hope:

> But when expressive rupture takes place, repetition becomes a process of creative assemblage, forging new incorporeal objects, new "abstract machines." (cited in Moreland, 8)

Such a new assemblage means, in this context, the extension of Twain's "realist" approach to include "incorporeal objects" in the form of "real" ghosts, such as the ghost of Beloved, which energizes a new pedagogical situation—"a new condition of knowledge" (Felman 1987, 31). For example, the elaborate lies with which Huck hopes to protect Jim can now be read as "creative assemblages" in the context of Morrison's rereading. "Lies" that Huck tells are in the service of a larger social truth, the discovery of which can now be seen as a "work in progress" (Moreland 1991, 12) that requires "new codes of love" (Kristeva cited in Moreland, 12).

> The elaboration of both negative and positive freedoms in a discourse of love is a "work in progress" more easily traced in Twain's novel thanks to the similarly new and particular codes of love elaborated still farther and more explicitly in Morrison's novel between another runaway slave in Sethe and another young poor-white runaway who helps her in Amy Denver. (12)

It has been said of the American South that we are obsessed with the past, but that it is a romanticized mythical past that we remember and as such is ahistorical. Still, our history presents itself in daily life in hidden ways. It surfaces in the form of violence and guilt that some theorists say is peculiar to the South. We seem torn between what W. J. Cash called a "frontier" mentality of radical individualism and what are sometimes suffocating community ties (1969). If this is so, and we suffer from a repression of collective memory as a society, perhaps the South needs a kind of social psychoanalysis, as Pinar has suggested (1991), and perhaps novelists, as I have taken some effort so far to suggest, are capable of being an important part of that analysis.

Twain seems to be addressing the well-worn conflict between radical individualism and community responsibility that takes a particular form in the South. He does this, according to Richard Gray, by "dissecting the Southern myths and exposing their faults and weaknesses" (1986, 115). However, Jim's story is not told and, at the end of *Adventures of Huckleberry Finn*, Gray suggests that Twain seems even to give up on his hero. As Gray states:

> Huck is pushed to one side of the action, Tom Sawyer is permitted to
> play his familiar games, and the issue of Jim's slavery is reduced to the
> level of farce. For all Huck's occasional protests at Tom's behaviour,
> or his famous final cry of defiance, the comedy loses its edge, the
> moral problems are minimized. (115)

As discussed above, Ellison disagrees with this reading. Here is where, perhaps, Morrison picks up the story one hundred years after Twain, and fifty years after Ellison.

Just as Sethe, Paul D., and Denver begin to trust in the possibility of a new life together, the past comes back to haunt them in such a way that they cannot dismiss it. Similarly, a blocked reading of *Adventures of Huckleberry Finn*, and perhaps other Southern literature, might lull us into complacency before fully confronting our repressed past. Morrison teaches us (as, Ellison points out, Twain alluded to but was unable to teach us directly) that past suffering can be most scarring when it is repressed. Confronted, that repressed past can become a source of wisdom—wisdom that may otherwise be unattainable. (A "line of flight" from structures that oppress is hollow without a preliminary and ongoing inner search.)

Huck's painful childhood experiences take him on a line of flight of often solitary excitement and adventure. But, one might ask, where is Jim's "line of flight"? Huck is able to do this because he has discovered his "invisibility" in a social and historical moment when a young white boy on a raft is not particularly noticeable. This assurance of a kind of invisibility affords him a freedom of movement not available to a black runaway slave. Ellison is able to discover the benefits of such invisibility only because his character lives in mid-twentieth century inner-city New York. But, as Nadel explains, "Ellison's imagery highlights the dilemma of which both he and Twain were well aware—that there was no place for Jim to go" (1988, 132). As Morrison's story reveals, the most marginalized are able to attain a "line of flight" of sorts only through an internal search coupled with the assistance and cooperation of a community. Invisibility of the sort that Huck (and later, Invisible Man) is able to utilize is unavailable to Jim or Sethe or Paul D. On the other hand, Huck seems less able to look inward than are, ultimately, Morrison's characters.

Still, this inner search in which a repressed past is exhumed is not without danger. The past can take over the present as it did for a time in *Beloved* when Denver had to shift her protective efforts from Beloved to Sethe (as did the rest of the community). Southern ahistorical obsession with the past must be confronted with history in order to overcome obsessiveness. That history lives in the present, in part, *through* that obsessiveness. But when love (such as Sethe's love for Beloved) and historical consciousness become overwhelmed by guilt, growth is no longer possible. In order to be a mobilizing force the past must be exorcised from dwelling under the skin, so to speak, but not from conscious memory. The ambiguously positive ending for *Beloved* seems to hold the possibility of that promise both for the novel's characters as well as the reader.

Examples of pasts that dwell under the skin are manifested by irony, cynicism, and guilt, and can be found scattered throughout Faulkner's *Absalom, Absalom!* This manner of approach to history points to particular approaches to theory as well. Visual metaphors in *Invisible Man* are gathered around the notion of a gaze that intends to control by way of surveillance—a gaze that does not really "see" anyone, least of all itself. "Outside the Brotherhood we were outside history; but inside of it they didn't see us" (Ellison 1952, 488). Attention is directed, via Ellison's brightly lit and illegally electrified city basement filled with jazz and blues sounds, toward the ways in which "official" written history (including literary theories) means to control, as well as toward that which it cannot control—the criminal, the schizophrenic, the marginal, the noisy, the invisible, the perverse, the phantasm. Ellison's writing highlights the possibilities for a different approach to social, historical, and literary theories—a point made by Eamon Halpin in his essay "The Ocular and the Otic: Theoretical Paradigms in Faulkner and Ellison" (1990). The generation of alternative theoretical possibilities is yet one more way in which literature translates tradition. In this case the translation is noted by Halpin to occur between Ellison and Faulkner.

A "social theory" which "sees" itself (that is, is aware of its own complicity in the knowledge it produces) is very different from theory that underpins the Brotherhood or theory that emerges, as Halpin notes, from a particular reading of Faulkner's *Absalom, Absalom!* Literary (and other) theories which are "visual"—that is, they represent an all seeing eye/"I"—are compared to literary theories provoked by Ellison's writing. The sense in which Ellison's writing exhibits a different—in some senses opposite—literary theoretical paradigm from that displayed in *Absalom, Absalom!* is another way in which his novel "converses" with Faulkner.

Faulkner's Rosa Coldfield is obsessed. She wants to know—wants to control—the way the story of Sutpen's Hundred, and of Thomas Sutpen himself, gets told and is received. Rosa repeats to a reluctant young local man, Quentin Compson, her story of the past in the small Mississippi town where she lives and where, years earlier, a stranger who moved there disrupted her life. Rosa is not the only one who is repeating the story, but it is her version which dominates the novel in its excessively personal, hyperbolic, and paranoid tone. She resembles the literary critic in the sense that in her living of her story, "her condition is one of belatedness" (6). Her "methodology is a hermeneutics of suspicion. . . . For Rosa meaning is always concealed, lurking in secrecy and guilt beneath an illusory surface" (7). "Her role in the novel's events is one of surveillance" (8). Like Ellison's Brotherhood, Rosa believes herself able to see things in others that others cannot see for themselves.

> Her penetrating vision allows her, or at least seems to allow her, to occupy a position of greater power than either Ellen [Rosa's sister who married Sutpen] or her children, whom she tends to see as hapless victims. Their visibility is the opposite of Rosa's own condition, which is a kind of invisibility. Rosa sees but for the most part cannot be seen herself. (8)

In her monumental efforts to know, she exemplifies Lyotard's description of the "opposition between scientific and narrative knowledge" (Halpin 1990, 10):

> The scientist questions the validity of narrative statements and concludes that they are never subject to argumentation or proof. He

classifies them as belonging to a different mentality: savage, primitive, underdeveloped, backward, alienated, composed of opinions, customs, authority, prejudice, ignorance, ideology. Narratives are fables, myths, legends, *fit only for women and children.* (cited in Halpin, 10, emphasis added)

As such, Rosa's approach to interpretation operates within a complicated opposition of scientific objectivity versus superstition or narrative knowledge, and masculinist versus feminist, adult versus child. She—"almost despite herself—provides us with an insight into the profoundly interested nature of interpretive and critical discourse. In her the scientific observer is exposed as a kind of paranoid voyeur or spy" (Halpin 1990, 10). For Halpin, Rosa represents the paradigm of modernist literary criticism.

Ellison's Invisible Man, on the other hand, in feeling victimized by the paradigm of this interpretive strategy, begins to look for alternatives—alternative subjectivities. While at times he responds to his victimization in kind—that is, by using his own invisibility as a means of "power or control over those who can be seen" (16)—at other moments his invisibility seems creative of a movement away from static, asymmetric, and violent power relations. Here,

invisibility seems to offer him a path to a different kind of subjectivity, a subjectivity which is not linked to the omniscient eye, but to the unpredictable and unbounded reverberation, to echoes and acoustics, to sound and music. (16)

This "music of invisibility" signals an alternative "experimental subjectivity" which the subject is able to move into or out of "at any point" (17). "The subject is never quite in time, never part of a regular and predictable beat within which it could feel in full control of itself and its destiny" (17). Such an experimental subjectivity, by virtue of the fact that it is "experimental," is inherently aware of its own complicity in positioning. It is "invisible, not blind" (Ellison 1952, 563). Invisible Man seems to find considerable power at last through his awareness of his invisibility—invisibility which he says is not the same thing as blindness such as Jack's (of the Brotherhood). This awareness is brought into "sharp focus" when Invisible Man is forced to leap outside history in a very literal sense as he burns the papers signifying his own history in search of light and escape from a manhole. This idea is extended in the epilogue when he says, "so after years of trying to adopt the opinions of others I finally rebelled. I am an Invisible Man" (560).

Still, to fall (or jump) into a hole never to emerge is to respond to blindness with blindness—merely a response in kind. "The politics of infinitely advancing while looking over the shoulder is a very dangerous exercise. You tend to fall into a hole" (Stuart Hall 1987, 45).

Fit Only for Women and Children

While Rosa's narrative strategy may indeed offer insight into the paranoia of much modernist criticism, her own story comes through in another manner—a manner that points to the significance of absences, in terms of race and gender, in this novel. For me, the most intriguing absences are the voices of Judith (Rosa's niece, Sutpen's daughter) and Clytie (Sutpen's mulatto daughter and slave), while the most intriguing presence is the voice of Rosa. All three are powerful characters who are crucial to the novel. Still, Rosa has the only female voice, and that voice is represented as near hysteria. The relationship between Rosa and Clytie strikes me as the most complex and perhaps the most suggestive.

It seems to me that the complexities, ambiguities, and psychology of racism, Southern racism in particular, are most significantly explored through these female characters. And through exploration of racism, the perhaps more universal themes of love, hate, and sexuality are confronted in their particularistic, Southern regional forms. Rosa is clearly obsessed with the Sutpen family in general, Sutpen in particular, and appears to live vicariously through them even after their deaths. This apparent preoccupation with Thomas Sutpen gets projected onto Clytie after the death of Charles Bon (Judith's mulatto half-brother, unbeknownst to Judith, and lover)—a death of one who represents for Rosa her own potential for love and passion as expressed through her "summer of wistaria" at age fourteen. (Rosa's erotic fantasizing in her "summer of wistaria" is reminiscent of Hurston's Janie and her "pear tree in bloom.") Indeed it is Clytie's physical touch, "touch of flesh with flesh which abrogates, cuts sharp and straight across the devious intricate channels of decorous ordering, which enemies as well as lovers know because it makes them both" (Faulkner 1936, 139), that shocks Rosa into an awareness of the tangled knot of race, sex, love, and hate. Awareness, however, does not constitute understanding. Minrose Gwin in her book *Black and White Women of the Old South* expresses Rosa's awareness-without-understanding as follows:

> Rosa's driving need is not so much to discover the nature of the "something . . . living hidden in that house," but to know herself—to understand why her life has turned out as it has. She finds in Clytie an objective correlative for the intense ambivalence, the love and the hate, she feels for herself as white southern woman trapped by gender, history, culture, and her own racism. Rosa may intuit Clytie as a female shadow-self, the product of pure sexual passion which young Rosa envisions, but never experiences. (1985, 117)

According to Catherine Clement (and her reading of Freud), a collective repressed past survives in the hysterical woman more than in anyone else (1988, 3–39). Rosa's hysteria certainly seems to bear that out in this novel, where it takes the form of a paranoia that is exemplary of the entire South in many ways. In paranoia, according to Paul Smith, "the 'subject' thus endows the external world with what it takes to be its own worst tendencies and qualities. . . . [Projection] is undertaken in order to maintain the fiction, exactly, of a wholeness and wholesomeness in the subjects' internal economy" (1988, 95–96). "Rosa reflects the darkness of the white self which rejects human connection with the black Other" (Gwin 1985, 111). As one defines oneself, in part, by who one defines as other, this division and destruction of the racial other is division and destruction of the self. It is a self divided against itself. Indeed, it is the relationship between Clytie and

Rosa which finally destroys them both. Rosa's noted tendency toward an interpretation through the gaze, or a hermeneutics of suspicion, could be thought of as a kind of hysterical male identification. Could Faulkner write her otherwise than "male"? She is the only extensively articulated woman.

These "silences" are indeed noisy. Either the women are great gossips, paranoid, obsessed, and with no life, or they are stunned into silence. The silent ones are somehow saintly and surreal. Nevertheless, his narrative leads us to speculate on a vast and complex interiority to women and black people, even though such is not provided overtly. In Zora Neale Hurston's novel *Their Eyes Were Watching God*, published just one year after *Absalom, Absalom!*, we see a "corrective" to missing black speech, black female speech in particular.

The historical moment among the black literati in which Hurston wrote *Their Eyes Were Watching God* was one of contestation over what constitutes an appropriate tone in black writing. Hurston was in the minority as one who wrote in "dialect" and as one whose work was not directly preoccupied by black struggles with racism. One of her most vociferous critics was Richard Wright, who felt her lack of bitterness toward whites and the "minstrel image" her work perpetuated were counter-revolutionary (Hemenway 1977, 241).

Hurston wanted her work to be far-removed from what she called "the sobbing school of Negrohood," (220) and claimed that such writing was even a distortion: "We talk about the race problem a great deal, but go on living and laughing and striving like everybody else" (221). Hemenway expands on this thought in his biography of Hurston.

> By leaving out "the problem," by emphasizing the art in the folkloric phenomenon, Hurston implicitly told whites: Contrary to your arrogant assumptions, you have not really affected us that much; we continue to practice our own culture, which as a matter of fact is more alive, more esthetically pleasing than your own; and it is not solely a product of defensive reactions to your actions. She felt that black culture manifested an independent esthetic system that could be discussed without constant reference to white oppression. The

price for this philosophy was an appearance of political naiveté and the absence of an immediate historical presence. (221)

Still, as Michael Cooke (1984) points out, there is a potential regressiveness to particular forms and/or timing for Signifyin(g), a major trope for *Their Eyes Were Watching God.* (I will return to this later as I introduce Jamaica Kincaid's writing.)

Hurston's novel begins with "definitions" of men's desire (which, according to Gates [1988], is a revision of, or Signifyin(g) on, Frederick Douglas's 1845 text) and women's desire opposed to one another, and which Hurston reverses later within the text. She characterizes men as "watchers" of distant ships, and women as "dreamers" creating their own "truth" (lives), and then reverses this as the protagonist's (Janie's) grandmother (Nanny) talks about the distant ship carrying her dreams, whereas Tea Cake (Janie's third husband) sees the distant ship, and all else that has to do with his fate, as under his control. This reversal is ever-reversing throughout the text—those "definitions" never stable.

Broadly speaking, the text is the story of a black woman in search of self-awareness, which is "thematize[d] through an opposition between the inside and the outside of things" (Gates 1988, 184)—or, a kind of divided self. The advantages to keeping things (self) divided, as referred to by Ellison's Invisible Man, are strikingly demonstrated in *Their Eyes Were Watching God* and brilliantly interpreted by Barbara Johnson (1987).

Johnson recalls Jakobson's discovery of patterns of aphasia (loss or partial loss of speech) as falling into two main categories: similarity disorders and contiguity disorders. With such disorders the ability to follow one topic from another on the basis of its similarity or contiguity is restricted or totally blocked. Personality, cultural style, and verbal style in "normal" (that is, nonaphasic) verbal behavior—behavior where both processes are continually operative—will exhibit preference for one process over the other, but some facility with both is necessary. One with a similarity disorder is unable to follow one topic from another *metaphorically;* with a contiguity disorder, one is unable to follow one topic with another *metonymically.*

Johnson points out, as has Paul de Man, that metaphor is the privileged trope of the two in Western culture, and together metaphor and metonymy constitute an interdependent opposition. Metaphor as a kind of analogy presents a necessity—an inference of identity and totality. Metonymy, because it has to do with contiguity, is perceived as coming about through chance—it is purely relational. One problem with this distinction—a problem that is highlighted by Hurston's use of these tropes—is that it is often difficult to tell the two tropes apart, as, for example, in "birds of a feather flock together" (those who are *alike* one another remain *next to* one another). This proverb sums up

> the tendency of contiguity to become overlaid by similarity, and vice versa. . . . One has only to think of the applicability of this proverb to the composition of neighborhoods in America to realize that the question of the separability of similarity from contiguity may have considerable political implications. (Johnson, B. 1987, 157)

Johnson demonstrates how Hurston is "acutely conscious of, and superbly skilled in, the seductiveness and complexity of metaphor as privileged trope and trope of privilege" (159) through her analysis of the following passage from *Their Eyes Were Watching God*. In the text, the passage follows an argument between Janie and her second husband, Joe Starks, over her handling of a business matter in their store. Joe tells Janie that "Somebody got to think for women and chillun and chickens and cows" (cited in Johnson, 159) as they cannot think for themselves.

> Times and scenes like that put Janie to thinking about the inside state of her marriage. Time came when she fought back with her tongue as best she could, but it didn't do her any good. It just made Joe do more. He wanted her submission and he'd keep on fighting until he felt he had it.
> So gradually, she pressed her teeth together and learned how to hush. The spirit of the marriage left the bedroom and took to living in the parlor. It was there to shake hands whenever company came to visit, but it never went back inside the bedroom again. (Hurston 1978, 55)

Janie's thoughts at this time take her back to an incident which revealed to her that "She wasn't petal-open anymore with him" (56). Joe had slapped and berated her after she had ruined a meal.

> Janie stood where he left her for unmeasured time and thought. She stood there until something fell off the shelf inside her. Then she went inside there to see what it was. It was her image of Jody tumbled down and shattered. But looking at it she saw that it never was the flesh and blood figure of her dreams. Just something she had grabbed up to drape her dreams over. In a way she turned her back upon the image where it lay and looked further. She had no more blossomy openings dusting pollen over her man, neither any glistening young fruit where the petals used to be. . . . She had an inside and an outside now and suddenly she knew how not to mix them. (cited in Johnson, B. 1987, 161–62)

Janie's self-division into her inside/outside opposition is expressed through her use and reversals of the metaphor/metonymy opposition. Her marriage situation is related to metaphorically, analogically, as the house and the store. Her marriage space is related to metonymically, "a movement through a series of contiguous rooms" (163). In the first paragraph of the passage where "the spirit of the marriage left the bedroom, [there is an] externalization of the inner, metaphorically grounded in metonymy" (163). "Something fell off the shelf inside her" (163), in the second paragraph, reveals an "internalization of the outer, metonymically grounded metaphor" (163).

> The reversals operated by the chiasmas [above] map out a reversal of the power relations between Janie and Joe. Henceforth, Janie will grow in power and resistance, while Joe deteriorates both in his body and in his public image. (163)

At the point which Janie realizes "how not to mix them," she also acquires the power of voice. This power "grows not out of her identity but out of her division into inside and outside" (163). The ability to articulate, to have "the power of voice," requires this division in figurative language—the simultaneous presence of distinct poles, inside and outside, similarity and contiguity, metaphor and metonymy, and "not their collapse into oneness" (163). But *distinct* does not mean that such poles can be spoken outside one another. It should be reiterated that a peculiar characteristic of hierarchical oppositions is their interdependence upon one another. This division, therefore, *requires deconstruction* for its "resolution," not dialectical synthesis.

> It must be remembered that what is at stake in the maintenance of both sides [as divided]—metaphor and metonymy, inside and outside—is the very possibility of speaking at all. The reduction of a discourse to oneness, identity—in Janie's case, the reduction of woman to mayor's wife—has as its necessary consequence aphasia, silence, the loss of ability to speak: "She pressed her teeth together and learned to hush." (164)

There is a difference, then, between self-division that is divided *against* the self—a *difference within* that creates frustration, hatred, xenophobia, "sick" schizophrenia, neurosis, division that is a sort of surgical cutting off between self and other as in Lacan's mirror stage—and self-division that is *for* the "self"—division that enables voice, prevents (critical) aphasia, avoids essentialist collapsing of differences. Deconstructive difference and deferral of understanding is the very basis of understanding anything at all here.

It is only through a faith in and seeking of love that Janie is moved to action, to speech, moved to learn. And it is finally through the realization of the love she sought (with her third husband, Tea Cake) that Janie gains the self-knowledge required to understand a history that lives in the present.

> Dis is uh love game. Ah done lived Grandma's way, now Ah means tuh live mine. . . . She was borned in slavery time when folks, dat is black folks, didn't sit down anytime dey felt lak it. So sittin' on porches lak de white madam looked lak uh mighty fine thing tuh her. Dat's whut she wanted for me—don't keer whut it cost. Git up on uh high chair and sit there. She didn't have time tuh think whut tuh do after you got up on de stool uh do nothin'. De object wuz tuh git dere. So

> Ah got up on de high stool lak she told me, but Pheoby, Ah done
> nearly languished tuh death up dere. Ah felt like de world wuz cryin'
> extry and Ah ain't read de common news yet. (Hurston 1978, 171–72)

The story ends with her in relative solitude (what Cooke calls
"accomplished solitude" [1984, 84]), reflecting the way Hurston's own
life-story ended. But it is a different solitude than that of Invisible
Man, who has yet to sustain an intimate relationship with anyone. Still,
Janie's intimacy has been limited, for the most part, to one other. Her
friendship with Pheoby signals hope for her connection to the community—a connection that she desired earlier but that was largely stifled
by Joe Starks. Tea Cake stifled this connection in his own way as well.
It was he who convinced Janie he could be trusted to return from long
absences from her, yet it was also he who could not stand, eventually,
to allow her out of his sight.

This love for her reached its pinnacle with his madness. Bitten by a
rabid dog, he was "mad with love," jealous to the point of murder, at
which time Janie shot him in self defense. Once again Janie took control of her life by refusing to be canceled—this time by what may have
been becoming fusion love, although that possibility is steeped in a rich
ambiguity. The drama of this final scene is descriptive of the risk of
love, ambivalence of desire, the potential violence (though necessity) of
knowledge, of the pedagogical relationship. She chooses to sustain the
love she's known with Tea Cake through place and memory.

> So Ah'm back home agin and Ah'm satisfied tuh be heah. Ah done
> been tuh de horizon and back and now Ah kin set heah in mah house
> and live by comparisons. Dis house ain't so absent of things lak it
> used tuh be befo' Tea Cake come along. It's full uh thoughts, 'spe-
> cially dat bedroom. (Hurston 1978, 284)

Of Janie's ending in "accomplished solitude," her rejection of the
social sphere, Cooke writes, "Her home is a symbol of her condition,
free and proud and yet radically unshared" (1984, 84). Her solution is
to *choose* a kind of communal marginality.

She pulled in her horizon like a great fish-net. Pulled it from around the waist of the world and draped it over her shoulder. So much of life in its meshes! She called in her soul to come and see. (Hurston 1978, 286)

This rejection of the communal in favor of the individual is, as a personal solution, perhaps ironic for an author whose life-work was to preserve the community of African-American folk culture. Rather than view it, as Cooke does, as a rejection of all but solitude, a rejection of intimacy—an ironic and thus cynical turn—her refusal to sever herself from her past and the pedagogical situation she sets up between herself and Pheoby ("'Lawd!' Pheoby breathed out heavily, 'Ah done growed ten feet higher from jus' listenin' tuh you, Janie. Ah ain't satisfied wid mahself no mo'" [284]) could be thought to signal a beginning in her conclusion. The celebratory note with which Hurston ends the novel (Janie embraces all of the life within the mesh that is her horizon) is not a note of disconnection or isolation. It differs radically from Ellison's ending with Invisible Man still in the hole—albeit contemplating leaving that hole for love and social action. She did, after all, return to her community. It is hard to imagine that she came back there only to isolate herself from the others.

The power of the fictional register (of language) is recognized by her earlier in the novel as she "kills" Joe Starks with her words—an act of "motivated Signifyin(g)"—thereby avoiding her own cancellation and, further, creating her "self." Yet the strength of her words depended on the public, communal witnessing (and understanding) of their utterance. Her act of telling the tale, to herself, to Pheoby, signifies her recognition of the autobiographical register in forming identity.

Like Hurston, and in another sense Faulkner, Jamaica Kincaid's project consists of an exploration of self through discovering history that lives in the present. Much of the writing in *A Small Place* and *Lucy* proceeds through a discourse of anger. But to read her only as this is to miss the greater significance in her stories. One literary mode of expression for Kincaid, particularly in *Lucy*, is a *metissage*—"initiating a genuine dialogue with the dominant discourses they hope to transform, thus ultimately favoring exchange rather than provoking conflict"

(Lionnet 1989, 3). This mode of writing inherently presents a challenge to essentializing tendencies in the written history of Western culture. As such, as a literary mode and theoretical category, it holds some cultural specificity similar to the ways in which Signifyin(g) does. Its specificity, however, is not derivative of any one particular culture so much as it belongs to a notion of postcolonial culture.

The difference between this mode of writing and that of Signifyin' is in its directness. Both constitute a kind of translation and, in the case of "unmotivated Signifyin(g)" at least, a kind of dialogue. However, *metissage* conceived of as a "cultural braiding" does not necessarily proceed through chiasmus—repetition and reversal. It is this very *indirectness* in Signifyin(g) that sometimes renders it regressive rather than subversive or socially active and creative. As Cooke observes:

> Signifying always involves questions of power on two levels, the social and the mental, and the signifier is the one who as best he can makes up for a lack of social power with an exercise of intellectual or critical power. (1984, 26)

This strategy amounts to little or, at worst, it can backfire when one is

> busy signifying, but no one [can] tell. Signifying and wishful thinking tend to coincide here. Signifying becomes an idle secret and, as Gates has justly remarked, dangerously close to tomming. (29)

When, for example, a black artist "signifies on" white racial stereotype in certain ways and at certain times, "both black and white come out the worse" (29), the white for maintaining ignorant beliefs, "the black for playing not so much on as down to that belief" (29). Kincaid entertains no such play.

Jamaica Kincaid warns of the dangers of reading like a tourist—of pre(sub)suming a particular text, of mistranslating, of failing to remember one's own deep unknowing of the "known," the "native" in the text. We begin with her book *A Small Place* (1988) as a tourist (or would-be tourist) of Antigua who Kincaid hopes to teach. Later, in her book *Lucy* (1990), she comes to the United States as an *au pair* and finds us still mistranslating (even ourselves), or else not bothering to translate at all, placing the entire burden on the immigrant, choosing ignorance.

A Small Place is not called a novel. It is an essay about life among tourists, natives, and neocolonizers in "postcolonial" Antigua. However, I am struck by its similarities to her autobiographical fiction *Lucy*. Both are angry works. Kincaid, in an interview with Donna Perry, says she is through being "charming"—"when people say you're charming you are in deep trouble" (cited in Perry 1990, 498).

Kincaid plays with a kind of complete reversal of the colonizer/colonized or tourist/native hierarchies through her words of utter disdain for white tourists from England and North America. Tourists become for her the embodiment of all that is ugly, dirty, stupid and, in some senses, evil—characteristics colonizers typically ascribe to colonized.

> And you look at . . . the way they [Antiguans] squat down over a hole they have made in the ground, the hole itself is something to marvel at, and since you are being an ugly person this ugly but joyful thought will swell inside you: their ancestors were not clever in the way yours were and not ruthless in the way yours were, for then would it not be you who would be in harmony with nature and backwards in that charming way? An ugly thing, that is what you are when you become a tourist, an ugly, empty thing, a stupid thing, a piece of rubbish pausing here and there to gaze at this and taste that, and it will never occur to you that the people who inhabit the place in which you have just paused cannot stand you. (Kincaid 1988, 16–17)

This reversal is sustained almost throughout the entire text but with interludes for describing and explaining Antiguan internalization of oppressor *modus operandi* and values in postcolonial Antigua. Then, the last two sentences:

> Of course, the whole thing is, once you cease to be a master, once you throw off your master's yoke, you are no longer human rubbish, you are just a human being, and all the things that adds up to. So, too, with the slaves. Once they are no longer slaves, once they are free, they are no longer noble and exalted; they are just human beings. (81)

Kincaid's rage is most likely shocking to her (intended) readers (intended for the *New Yorker* magazine initially, but the first time any of her writing was ever rejected by it [Perry 1990, 497]). But the colonial history of Antigua lives in the present—undeniably for those subject to its excess. Antiguans, long since "emancipated," are still servants to foreigners and Antiguans corrupted by foreigners. Where else, Kincaid asks, could we have learned about capital, Gross National Product, and so on?

> I realized in writing that book that the first step to claiming yourself is anger. You get mad. And you can't do anything before you get angry. And I recommend getting very angry to everyone, anyone. (498)

For the sake of her arguments, she deploys essentialisms of both tourist and native: British, North American and Antiguan. In her last two novels (the ones examined here) she exhibits, at times, a bitterness toward all of the above that is quite different from novelistic approaches of African-Caribbean Wilson Harris. His novels, for example, could be said to be *themselves* a view or views to the transformations he imagines rather than didactics for the way to get there, or admonitions against obstacles to getting there. Some of Kincaid's earlier works (*At the Bottom of the River* [1978] and *Annie John* [1983]) could be said to more closely resemble what has been called Harris's "postmodern" or "poststructural" style (Covi 1990, 345–54). I have chosen, however, to deal only with the two most recent texts as Kincaid claims to have abandoned her older style for good, and as these two texts are such clear demonstrations of the ways repressed histories live—particularly through language:

> For isn't it odd that the only language I have in which to speak of this crime is the language of the criminal who committed the crime? And what can that really mean? For the language of the criminal can contain only the goodness of the criminal's deed. The language of the criminal can explain and express the deed only from the criminal's point of view. It cannot contain the horror of the deed, the injustice

of the deed, the agony, the humiliation inflicted on me. (Kincaid 1988, 31–32)

In this way her writing is a clear example of cross-cultural encounter as it reveals the operation of translation with a master.

The bitterness and anger remain in *Lucy*. However, she finds as Invisible Man discovered, "too much of your life will be lost, its meaning lost, unless you approach it as much through love as through hate" (Ellison 1952, 580). Lucy indeed loves Mariah, wife and mother in her *au pair* family, at the same time she is an astute observer of her foibles and contradictions and the connections of these to larger American society—to patriarchy, to commodification, to alienation and angst. It is toward these connections that Mariah seems oblivious except from a very limited "liberal feminist" and "liberal environmentalist" perspective.

> Mariah says, "I have Indian blood in me," and underneath everything I could swear she says it as if she were announcing her possession of a trophy. How do you get to be the sort of victor who can claim to be the vanquished also?
>
> I now heard Mariah say, "Well," and she let out a long breath, full of sadness, resignation, even dread. I looked at her; her face was miserable, tormented, ill-looking. She looked at me in a pleading way, as if asking for relief, and I looked back, my face and my eyes hard; no matter what, I would not give it. . . .
>
> I said, "How do you get to be that way?" The anguish on her face almost broke my heart, but I would not bend. It was hollow, my triumph, I could feel that, but I held on to it just the same. (Kincaid 1990, 40–41)

Mariah is unaware of the psychosocial and political dynamics of otherness. Yet Lucy loves Mariah's warmth and innocence at the same time she resents her seemingly willful ignorance. Lucy sees her own mother in Mariah—her mother being the major reason she left Antigua. Seeing her mother in Mariah seems to help Lucy to deal with her own contradictory feelings toward her. Through this love

Lucy and Mariah enter a pedagogical relationship in which both teach and learn.

The pedagogical imperative with which we are faced in Kincaid's work is that of cross-cultural imagination—literacy of the imagination—which includes a rereading of our own place in colonial history. It is not read as history *per se*, but more as history that lives in the present—much like Pinar's characterization of the repressed but living racial history (1993). One illustrative episode in *Lucy* is when Mariah takes Lucy to a favorite clearing in the woods in order to surprise her with the extravagant beauty of an entire field of blooming daffodils:

> "Mariah, do you realize that at ten years of age I had to learn by heart a long poem about some flowers I would not see in real life until I was nineteen?" . . . This woman who hardly knew me loved me, and she wanted me to love this thing—a grove brimming over with daffodils in bloom—that she loved also. Her eyes sank back in her head as if they were protecting themselves, as if they were taking a rest after some unexpected hard work. It wasn't her fault. It wasn't my fault. . . . The same thing could cause us to shed tears, but those tears would not taste the same. (Kincaid 1990, 30)

Both Kincaid and Wilson Harris write of West Indian children having to memorize Wordsworth's "I Wandered Lonely as a Cloud" (the daffodil poem). Both express a kind of ambivalence to the educational practice that is characteristic of Harris's notion of cross-cultural imagination—an ambivalence that is "unsettlement." As Harris explains:

> That unsettlement is rooted in paradox and in auction block histories, it is rooted in centuries of the conquest of species in nature, it is rooted in the conversion of conquistadorial biases into the humour of finity and infinity. Schoolchildren in the West Indies used to write quite naturally and innocently, it seemed, of English snow and Wordsworthian daffodils that they had never seen, rather than palm-groves or cane-fields or rainforests. The absurdity has often (and rightly so) been quoted as a caveat of blindness inculcated by colonial institutions stereotyped and bound within other cultural landscapes. (1983, 134)

What Harris calls the "unconscious infinity of humour" (134) results in West Indian writing that grew out of such schooling in which, for example, in a poem called *Snows* by Martiniquan poet St.-John Perse, "'strange alliances . . . white nuptials of noctuids, white festivals of mayflies' may come into attunement, on cross-cultural loom" (134) with poets and poems of other cultural and natural landscapes.

Kincaid's ambivalence about learning the Wordsworth poem, and other items from the British canon, is expressed in her interview with Perry:

> Every colonial child has to do that. It's a two-edged thing because I wouldn't have known how to write and how to think if I hadn't read those things. I wouldn't have known my idea of justice if I hadn't read *Paradise Lost*, if I hadn't been given parts of *Paradise Lost* to memorize. It was given to me because I was supposed to be Satan. The last chapter of the book I have written has a lot of things about that. The book is called *Lucy*, short for Lucifer. (1990, 507)

Kincaid reads history from a multifaceted perspective. Columbus's "discovery" of Antigua in 1493 fascinates her, and she sees it from the perspective of the poetics of exploration as well as the way that this "great curiosity in every human being [is] . . . bound up in this horrible thing that happened (slavery—the domination)" (cited in Perry, 501). Indeed, her approach to studying history generally is through studies of domination. While angry at the abominations, Kincaid sees no simple "solutions": "If you remove the apparatus for the game [of domination as a game of musical chairs] to go on, then permanently sitting down is its own prison" (cited in Perry, 501). "There's no such thing as a fresh start" (cited in Perry, 502).

Kincaid writes autobiographical fiction. As will be shown in the next chapter some theorists would claim all autobiography is fiction and/or all fiction is a kind of autobiography. I go to that chapter now to explore my own and some of my students' connections to those (uneasy) relations—relations displayed and disturbed by theoretical and literary readings that have gone before. These readings and writings subvert the curricula of "official knowledge" both in their challenges to textbook stories and in their manners of looking/ speaking. That challenge is addressed to every level of the educational enterprise.

5

Autobiographical
Heirs (Airs)

CULTURAL STUDIES AND THE SELF

In Plato's writings, dialogue gave way to the literary pseudodialogue. But by the Hellenistic age, writing prevailed, and real dialectic passed to correspondence. Taking care of oneself became linked to constant writing activity. The self is something to write about, a theme or object (subject) of writing activity. That is not a modern trait born of the Reformation or of romanticism; it is one of the most ancient Western traditions. It was well established and deeply rooted when Augustine started his Confessions.
—Michel Foucault, 1988

On one level this paper is a critique of other approaches. Written in a detached, disembodied voice, the paper masked me with a particular identity—that of the one whose approach was not simple or flawed, that of the one-who-knows. Wanting to stake out a place in the discussion on multicultural and antibias education, I took an aggressive position; that is, I tried to reveal the flaws in other approaches. I defined myself against everyone rather than in relation to anyone and collapsed myself onto an observing eye/I, and thus my identity as the one-who-knows became fixed.
—Peter Taubman, 1993

T HE AUTOBIOGRAPHICAL URGE is a strong one, I gather, from what
students, colleagues, and others have produced.[1] But just as there
are many ways to tell a story, there are many autobiographical forms
and approaches: there is memoir; exploration that is communal, that is,
autobiography written to represent an individual as a member of a
group; exploration that is psychosocial; "intellectual autobiography"
(Gorra 1995); and surely many others. Most autobiographical writing I
have seen is a combination, though the emphasized form varies. Being
compelled by a cultural studies project, it is important to me that I con-
vey my passion for autobiography framed within social-historical
contexts as well as within psycho-philosophical journeying. I prefer, in
most cases, that memoir be avoided altogether. Memoirs are the types
of stories we tell strangers about ourselves—stories that require the
least of us. However, memoir is the most familiar notion of self-writ-
ing. By attending to theorizing about autobiography, identity, and the
Self, the horizon of possibility expands for "reading and writing the
self" (Graham 1991).

Autobiography as a "genre" has been a theoretical problem for literary critics from the first appearances of critical literature about
autobiography, and contemporary theory is no exception (although the
way the problem is framed is often very different now) (Olney 1980,
3–27). It has been argued that, (a) all autobiography is fiction because
even the "self" is a fiction (Sprinker 1980), (b) autobiography provides
"truths" that nothing else does (Olney 1980, 13), (c) all historical and
autobiographical writing contains elements of fiction and elements of
fact or at least "truth" (Kerby 1988), (d) autobiography, or the writ-
ing/written self, is represented metaphorically by style (Starobinski
1980/1976), (e) autobiography exists only as "the late product of a specific civilization" (Gusdorf 1956/1980, 29), one which holds "conscious
awareness of the singularity of each individual life" (29) as opposed to
those societies/cultures that exist as interdependent communities.

For curriculum theorists Jacques Daignault and Clermont Gauthier
(1981) the search for identity—which is what autobiography may be
thought to be—is a search for a moving target. As such, the search
reveals a "paradox of sense" (180) that is within the "paradigm of infinite
regression" (180). "For example, in order to define a phenomenon we

use words but these words also need to be defined and the words used in these definitions need to be defined too and this infinitely" (180). The search is a game that never ends. Writing an "autobiography" would seem to be a way of saying "Here I am; the search is over," if autobiography is conceived as discovery of the self, or even, in some senses, as creation of a "completed" self. It is these conceptions of autobiography that Daignault's and Gauthier's paradoxical identity challenge.

Michael Sprinker, in his essay "Fictions of the Self: The End of Autobiography" (1980), echoes the above ideas about identity, making his case for the implications of this for autobiography through selected writings and discussions of Vico, Kierkegaard, Nietzsche, and Freud. He recounts stories from Kierkegaard's texts *Repetition* and *Fear and Trembling*, both written under pseudonyms, to assert their resemblance to Kierkegaard's own life. One of these texts is told "through a re-creation of Abraham's sacrifice of Isaac" (*Fear and Trembling*), and the other "through the fictional narrative of the relations between Constantius and the nameless young lover" (330). Some time later, Kierkegaard admitted to assuming the pseudonyms but denied having uttered any of the words written under them. In this way Kierkegaard

> refuses to assume the traditional responsibility of an author for his text, and in so doing he undermines the conventional notions of author and text, self and discourse. (332)

After noting this example of Kierkegaard's condition of writing as an intertextual "multiplicity of subjects" (332), Sprinker offers a reminder of Nietzsche's "obliterat[ion of] the authority of the subject by exposing it as a deception" (334)—a deception designed to cover over the only "real" authority: the will to power. The will to power, Nietzsche warns, is precisely what may drive one, in the name of autobiography, to find it "useful and important for one's activity to interpret oneself falsely" (cited in Sprinker, 334).

Freud took this admonition seriously in writing psychoanalysis, but Freud also serves, for Sprinker, as another personal example of one whose life demonstrates the ways in which "the life and the thought are, in fact, produced in the writing" (337).

> To turn Freud back upon himself [as did Lacan] is to discover a discourse trapped in its own discursiveness, or to put it another way, it is to discover in Freud a neurotic impulse to uncover the secrets and mechanisms of neurosis. (336)

And through an extended reading of Freud's *Interpretation of Dreams*, Sprinker draws an analogy from dream (text) interpretation and autobiography whereby both interpretation and "inquiry of the self into its own origin and history" always "return to confirm" themselves (342). That is, autobiography

> is always circumscribed by the limiting conditions of writing, of the production of a text. Vico, Kierkegaard, and Nietzsche all contend that the self is constituted by a discourse that it never completely masters. (342)

This last line is reminiscent of Felman's reading of Lacan's reading of Freud, where she finds the pedagogical imperative implicit in their work to be for a knowledge that is not in mastery of itself, that does not know what it knows (Felman 1982). Like any other knowledge, self-knowledge is only that which has discovered "that this master text, the unconscious, is perpetually changing" (Sprinker 1980, 342), Daignault's and Gauthier's paradoxical "search for identity" (1981), truly an "identity-in-motion" (Taubman 1993). The necessary intertextuality implied by Sprinker's "multiplicity of [writing] subjects" (1980, 332) is also reminiscent of Francois Lionnet's *metissage*, which is "a reading practice that allows me to bring out the interreferential nature of a particular set of texts" (1989, 8).

Sprinker was criticized by James Olney for his "Fictions of the Self" in the volume of collected essays in which Sprinker's essay appears (a collection edited by Olney). In response to poststructuralists in general, Sprinker in particular, Olney admonishes:

> what they are still troubling about is the self and consciousness or knowledge of it, even though in a kind of bravura way some of them may be denying rather than affirming its reality or its possibility. And

this is the crux of the matter, the heart of the explanation for the special appeal of autobiography to students of literature in recent times:
it is a fascination with the self and its profound, its endless mysteries
and, accompanying that fascination, an anxiety about the self, an anxiety about the dimness and vulnerability of that entity that no one has
ever seen or touched or tasted. (1980, 23)

Olney's critique was, in fact, prophetic, as more and more poststructuralist literary and cultural critics are now themselves producing
autobiographies (Gorra 1995).

In *Autobiography: Toward a Poetics of Experience*, Janet Varner Gunn
also criticizes Sprinker's essay for its poststructuralist underpinnings:

Drawing on the work of Jacques Lacan, Michel Foucault, and Jacques
Derrida, his essay joins autobiography to the ranks of *livres sans
auteurs*. The struggle against writing's law of gravity is finally in vain,
since "no autobiography can take place except within the boundaries
of a writing where concepts of subject, self, and author collapse into
the act of producing a text" [Sprinker, 342]. . . . For Sprinker, the
"self-written" cannot exist outside of [the text]. (Gunn 1982, 5–6)

I disagree with Gunn's interpretation of Sprinker and her implied interpretation of Derrida's famous proclamation, "there is nothing outside
the text" (Derrida 1976). The text to which she seems to refer is the particular autobiographical text. Perhaps a better translation of that
statement is Pagano's "there is nothing that is not a text" (1991, 202).
Apparently, Gunn and perhaps Olney read a pessimism into the idea that
what one writes about oneself is not reducible to that self or vice versa.

There is another critique to be directed toward Sprinker's essay,
however. While he writes of a "multiplicity of subjects" and intertextuality, he implies through his particular choice of examples and
discussions around them that this multiplicity is somehow still "centered," in a sense, within individual human beings. That is, there is no
sense of the cultural communal in his characterization of identity, writing, and autobiography. Autobiographies of the socially marginalized
emphasize (typically) a multiplicity that is also a plurality, a collectivity
of subjects and a collective subjectivity. It is this sort of intertextuality,

interreferentiality, intersubjectivity—a full and complex *metissage*—that is central to this study that Sprinker ignores, resists, or represses.

The above discussion is evocative of Olney's recognition (also in this collection) of some of the particular, popular uses of autobiography as "defining, organizing center[s]" (1980, 13) for various "studies," such as American Studies, Black Studies, Women's Studies, and African Studies.

> According to the argument of these critics (who are becoming more numerous every day), autobiography—the story of a distinctive culture written in individual characters and from within—offers a privileged access to an experience . . . that no other variety of writing can offer. (1980, 13)

However, Gusdorf, in his 1956 essay that is often credited with beginning modern autobiography criticism, paints autobiography as a fiercely individual act—a perspective that necessarily denies even the *possibility* of autobiography except insofar as it mirrors the dominant Western ideology of radical individualism.

> The author of an autobiography gives himself the job of narrating *his own* history; what he sets out to do is to reassemble the scattered elements of his *individual life* and to regroup them in a comprehensive sketch. . . . Autobiography . . . requires a *man* to take a distance with regard to himself in order to reconstitute himself in the focus of his *special unity* and identity across time. (1980, 35, emphases added)

For Shari Benstock, Gusdorf's way of defining and delimiting autobiography

> strikingly recapitulates the effects of Lacan's mirror stage . . . a recognition of the alienating force within the specular (the "regard") that leads to the desperate shoring-up of the reflected image against disintegration and division. (1988, 14–15)

Those, like Gusdorf, who reject, deny, or ignore the spirit of collectivity in the autobiographical act are searching for that which is a kind of "final authority," at least implicitly. As Pagano insists, such a search betrays a hunger for something outside, something beyond judgment according to which we might be absolutely certain—according to which any one of us might be the one presumed to know. This is, of course, the logic of domination. (1991, 201)

This self-authorized authoritative version of the subject, the self, is autobiography in which "the Subject is made an Object of investigation. . . . This view of the life history, is grounded in authority" (Benstock 1988, 19).

But just as with the conservative versus liberal or radical debates around culture and the humanities, discussed in chapter two, these issues and problems cannot be simply divided into polarized camps. This complexity is well illustrated in African-American autobiography, for example. African-American autobiography (beginning with slave narratives), in addition to questions around identity and subjectivity, has also to be thought through the context of who its expected audience has historically been, as well as its pedagogical imperative for that audience. Slave narratives were most often written to compel a white audience to abandon slavery. And much African-American autobiography since then has been directed at a *project* of antiracism. Of course, any autobiography must be thought through contextually in this manner, but I point to African-American autobiography in particular in order to highlight the very specific and often overlooked historical context of African-American writing. Often, in "writing the self into existence," authors from socially marginalized groups are also actively engaged in writing an entire people along with them. This alters the context for theorizing about autobiography from the apparent context for much white, Western autobiography theory. This context, with its larger pedagogical and emancipatory project, can render arguments about "fictions of the self" pedantic, but, at the same time, it renders the isolated, unified, "self-identical" self obsolete—a distortion. Somehow, the notion of a "fictional register" must be drawn into conversation with the communal and an autobiographical register.

Taubman has explored a notion identity through three registers. In the first register, identity emerges as a construct of language and, thus, as a kind of fiction which alienates one from the complex interplay of differences within oneself and between oneself and others. It can be viewed from a psychoanalytic perspective, as a result of Lacan's mirror stage. This fictional register functions through a self-essentializing movement in which boundaries between self and not-self, margin and center, are rigidly drawn and assumed stable. In this register, knowledge is discourse. An identity conceptualized from within this register alone may be understood by the way in which discursive practices "block understanding . . . or produce paranoid knowledge" (8). It is frozen within its own mirror image, mistaking the unity called "ego" as being synonymous with the subject.

The second register, which Taubman calls the "communal as an identity-in-motion" (9), involves group membership and all that it implies for identity as it emerges in the relations among and between individual, group, and society. The term "identity-in-motion" is derived from Gates's explanation of the "mask-in-motion," exemplified by the Yoruba mask which only produces meaning when worn in front of an audience of initiates. This meaning-making evokes a sense of interior cohesion for the group involved in the process of producing this meaning. Taubman explains:

> Within the communal register identity is made the ground for action. The identity is not taken as a formation of language but as an identity-in-motion. . . . In such a world only those who are members can explore the meaning of the identity. (10–11)

However, this register risks essentializing identity, freezing it into mere group membership if its relationship to other registers is lost.

The third register Taubman describes is the autobiographical. Explication of the subtle difference he intends between this register and the others requires that I quote him at length.

> Within the autobiographical register, unlike the fictional register, the narrative which the subject constructs does not create the real experience of living but rather posits the possibility of external validation. One's recounted autobiography therefore does not create one's experience but captures it. Thus autobiography as a means to self-knowledge

is possible since a dialectic exists between narrative and actual experience. This autobiography is both the ground for action and what is to be transformed. (14)

Within this register rests a vision for the possibility of responsibility, action, and agency from the perspective of transforming and transformative individuals in relationship to others. Nonetheless, as Taubman warns, there are dangers when this register loses sight of the others. Fixation within this register alone ignores the extent to which race, class, gender, ethnicity, and the unconscious do determine identity and knowledge. For example, a multicultural approach that is frozen in this register may take the position of a "color blind" curriculum. But it is also through this register in interaction and tension with the others that the operation of those multiple and partial determinisms may be explored. As Paul Valery reminds us, "There is no theory that is not a fragment, carefully prepared, of some autobiography" (cited in Lionnet 1989, 91).

The problem of the divided self that emerged through readings in chapter four resurfaces here. The self divided against itself is the self of the mirror stage—a stage which signals a search for unity that "derives from an experience of self as fragmented, partial, segmented, and different" (Benstock 1988, 12). It is a division between self and other which is experienced as absolute. And the self-division that is *for* the self is that which works through difference, thereby enabling voice, preventing a sort of critical aphasia or inability to distinguish and discriminate—learned illiteracy. Need is for the recognition of both divisions—re-cognition that is available only as the autobiographical register operates consciously within the context of the others. The deconstruction that takes place through this operation is eloquently described by Benstock:

If the autobiographical moment prepares for a meeting of "writing" and "selfhood," a coming together of method and subject matter, this destiny—like the retrospective glance that presumably initiates autobiography—is always deferred. Autobiography reveals gaps, and not only gaps in time and space or between the individual and the social, but also a widening divergence between the manner and matter of its discourse. That is, autobiography reveals the impossibility of its own dream: What begins on the presumption of self-knowledge ends in the creation of a fiction that covers over the premises of its construction. (11)

"Marginal" autobiography is in a unique position to come to this recognition. The fragmented, "postmodern self" that is so widely hailed as a (the?) "sign of the times," seems, in some senses, ludicrous to those whose communal histories have long known fragmentation, displacement, and dispossession in the most material senses as well as symbolic ones. W. E. B. DuBois's recognition brought to print of the "double consciousness" necessary for African-American survival and/or agency is an example (1969). As Stuart Hall explains:

> Identity is formed at the unstable point where the "unspeakable" stories of subjectivity meet the narratives of history, of a culture. And since he/she is positioned in relation to cultured narratives which have been profoundly expropriated the colonized subject is always "somewhere else": doubly marginalized, displaced always other than where he or she is, or is able to speak from. (1987, 44)

Our relations to such autobiographies (literatures), whether we are members of socially marginalized (colonized) groups or not, are extraordinarily significant to any notion of identity—both national and individual. Indeed our identities can only be thought through difference. It is only in our *relations* to others that identity, and thus autobiography, has meaning at all. Such a relational theory of autobiography guides my own autobiographical reading/rewriting of a novel (below) that I first read as an adolescent, and reread for this writing.

As Pinar implies, our autobiographical writing depends on our particular relations to marginality (1994, 218). Those of us who are indeed newly "victimized" as "fractured identities" within a particular (negative) facet of the "postmodern age," Christopher Lasch's "minimal self" (1984), need to attend to that self-division in our autobiographical constructions. Such a construction is what Pinar calls an "architecture"—a construction that takes seriously the boundaries one has erected as well as dissolved (1994). One who has not experienced what Hall calls "centering of marginality" (Hall 1987, 44), on the other hand, may benefit from abandoning "the image of an architecture of self" (Pinar, 395) for a deconstructed self. Hall's sentiments seem similar as he writes,

> I believe it is an immensely important gain when one recognizes that all identity is constructed across difference and begins to live with the politics of difference. But doesn't the acceptance of the fictional or narrative status of identity in relation to the world also require as a necessity, its opposite—the moment of arbitrary closure? Is it possible for there to be action or identity in the world without arbitrary closure—what one might call the necessity to meaning of the end of the sentence? (1987, 45)

Autobiography in Fiction

In another theoretical twist of the autobiographical matrix, rather than focusing on the fictional status of identity, theory also points toward the autobiographical, or "truthful," status of fiction. Kerby believes that history and autobiography ("self-narration") are necessarily narrative, and that this narrative does not exclude the "fictional." He expresses this notion as follows:

> Narrative truth may not do for an historical or biographical study that aims at "objectivity" (supposing this goal were even possible!), but it is, nevertheless, a curious fact of human reality that, to quote Ricoeur, "It makes little difference whether [the stories we tell] are true or false, fiction as well as verifiable history provides us with an identity." A "truthful" or "authentic" story of the human subject need not be one that achieves or even aims at objective historical verisimilitude. (1988, 238)

This position is not incompatible with Jean Starobinski's in the view that "truth" can be read from a text in ways unrelated to factual accuracy—for example, through "style" and through what is selected for narration. Since style is what distinguishes one author from another (one individual from another), style is the "essence" of autobiography and thus we cannot talk about the style of an autobiography or limit theory about it to genre.

> The conditions of autobiography furnish only a large framework within which a great variety of particular styles may occur. So it is essential to avoid speaking of an autobiographical "style" or even an autobiographical "form," because there is no such generic style or form. Here, even more than elsewhere, style is the act of an individual. (1980, 73)

In a similar sense, curriculum theorist Pagano makes pedagogical use of the self-narration that emerges from fictional writing of her students. They are, she suggests, much better able to expose their "desire for ignorance" (1991, 201) and thereby encounter the "surprise of otherness" through fictionalizing their journalizing of student teaching. In doing this "we go beyond ourselves" (202). Pagano expresses concern that in ("nonfictional") autobiographical writing, even that which is not to be graded, students may cover over their own "resistance to knowledge" or "desire to ignore" (201). In fictionalizing those accounts we are more inclined

> to probe our ignorances and to create new conditions for knowledge. . . . The advantage of fiction writing over autobiography is that the writer can claim a greater distance, and, consequently, the desire for ignorance is more readily exposed. (201)

Fictions allow one to write the ambiguity that is "identity"—"I am this, but not now; I was this, but not really." Jamaica Kincaid demonstrates this possibility, I think, in writing her novels as self-conscious autobiographies and her autobiography as fiction. Stories over the same chronological time sequences differ as she differs (and defers) from herself. Perspectives toward autobiography as self-authorized authoritative stories about ourselves that discover and unify the self remove us from relationality, politics, ultimately from meaning. These perspectives deny the active role of ignorance, the will to ignore. As Pagano suggests, fictional writing is one way to counter this.

The major issues in these arguments seem to revolve around subjectivity (What/where is it? If we do not know, can we even discuss autobiography?), the social and individual usefulness of autobiography, and the literary limits and functions of autobiography. If autobiography is fiction, does this mean that a project such as the one I suggest here is impossible and thus useless? That one cannot know more about the "self" in this way because one cannot write the "truth"? Or even, one cannot know more about the self because there is no unified "self" to know; the entity we call our "self" is so constantly in a state of flux that it makes no sense to attempt autobiography at all? Or that what we write exists only as a particular text and is not in the least representative of the "real" person who wrote it, or of anyone or anything at all aside from that particular text (it is a "thing-in-itself")?

It seems to me that there is a kind of truth to an affirmative answer to these questions, but that to leave it at that and dismiss autobiography misses the greater significance revealed in theoretical debates about identity and pedagogy. More to the point perhaps are the questions: Does it matter if this is "fact" or "fiction"? If it is all fiction, is there a "truth" in it? What is to be gained by doing this? Part of the "truth," I believe, lies in a negative answer to those earlier questions, and that is the part I am concerned with now. As Pinar understands, "we aim, in autobiography, at truthfulness, not truth, at expanding and complicating the lived space in which we dwell, through which we experience the world—as that space expands, so does the world to which we have access" (W. Pinar, personal communication, July 1991). Like most of the theorists mentioned above, I feel that much "truthfulness" lies completely outside the realm of the "factual." I also would argue that "truth" is contextually bound such that if I ask the question, "Is the self a fiction?" for one purpose, the answer might be the opposite of the reply to that same question when asked for a different purpose. This apparent opposition, then, is best dealt with in ways that mirror the apparent opposition between dialectical thinking and deconstruction (at least as I have set the two up in chapter three). A fictional/nonfictional self is a tension that moves, and its direction depends on the purposes behind its representation or articulation. Truthfulness is never expressed in only one way, as a block function. Reading the self with a literate imagination is surely at least as complex as good reading generally.

The particular "method" I am interested in for my own autobiographical writing in this chapter involves the interreferential reading of literature (autobiography, fiction, historical fiction) set in or near my own home or region, accompanied by reflective writing as a means of gaining insights into *self* and *other*, how I construct who the *other* is, how I am constructed as the *other*, and how a "sense of place" is itself built on notions of the *other*. Certain literary works can serve as highly accessible resources (as compared to so much of social theoretical literature) for reaching deeper understandings about the nuances of *difference* and *identity*. With such understandings, the possibilities for what could be called life-affirming and intelligent interpersonal relationships among teachers and students and their lives outside institutions are enhanced. Put another way, "repressed people tend to be stupid, and when smart, calculating only. Meditative, not just calculative, thought is an index of intelligence" (W. Pinar, personal communication, July 1991).

The concept of the *other* is a crucial one for understanding the construction of a *sense of place*. Creation of a notion of what constitutes *them and us*, the meaning derived from *difference*, of who, therefore, is *other* and the subsequent exclusion of the *other* (even within one's self) are often critical elements to the *sense of place*. (For example, think about the presumed mindset of one who is called "provincial," "local yokel," etc.)

Uncovering place in this way involves the process known to anthropologists as "making the familiar strange." This means, in the present context, rendering the strangeness of the *other*, which has been problematically made "familiar" through stereotyping and/or otherwise erasing, strange again though in a new sense of that term—a sense that does not assume strangeness to be frightening and hostile. The *other* is made strange in that the comforting familiarity of stereotyping is abandoned and replaced with the disturbing exhilaration that comes from exposing "dangerous remembrances" about past experiences that are contrary to "official" thought as it is so often written/spoken in conventional discourses—experiences which contribute to the present drama, often in unexpected ways. It means exploring and storying those "unique outcomes" as a foil against the dominant narratives that structure one's life.

Making the familiar strange also means, in this context, critically examining the cliches one has learned to live by—cliches which are not only expressed through language but also through routines, habits, ways of seeing. Where did they come from? What purposes have they served and do they serve? What happens when they are not taken for granted? Are my cliches the same order of reasoning as my stereotyping?

I see this approach as being useful for teacher education as, I believe, it is extremely important for teachers to be well-acquainted and comfortable with difference, including difference within themselves. This is important in that learning necessarily involves self-awareness, and self-awareness necessarily involves difference-awareness. How can teachers facilitate students' self discoveries and creations if teachers are unable to facilitate their own? Additionally, teachers and their relations (students, parents, public) stand to benefit immensely if teachers are equipped to examine their own desires—desires to teach, desires for students, desires for themselves. This acquaintance and comfort arises only after the *statues* that we have built of ourselves, those aspects of self trapped in, say, Lacan's Imaginary order, have been disturbed and rearticulated (Taubman 1993). Such a disturbance is made possible through, in part, intertextual readings of literary works and social and philosophical theory. In what may seem a paradoxical suggestion, the production of such readings are capable of disrupting the statue, yet such readings are only possible once disruption has begun. This is where autobiography, as an integral part of that intertextual adventure, becomes crucial. Through rereadings, rewritings, and re-visions, the situation (of reading and writing) moves, such that what at first appears as paradox is revealed to be closer to a hermeneutical process. Clearly, adaptations of this may be useful for teachers in a variety of classroom settings, but with the understanding that certain dangers inhere. Autobiography conceived narrowly, for example as only direct narrative confession, can be impositional and/or shattering for some students, or useless at best. This is why it is even more important to emphasize the notion, as Starobinski, Pagano, and as Kerby do, that autobiography can be conceived of as encompassing an almost endless variety of styles and approaches. One does not have to narrate some sort of "life story" in order to express/create/learn about ourselves honestly in writing.

In my classes, while I have not specifically asked for fictionalized autobiographies, students have been alerted to that possibility. Some have written poetry in response. One wrote a kind of poem that looped and circled around the pages, thereby expressing herself not only through word-signs but also spatially, in a kind of "topography." The primary place of fiction in my classroom has been, however, in the position of parallel readings—readings for students to respond to in their own autobiographical accounts. This has not always been done directly. Yet I have strongly sensed that those who read literary works in my classes were responding to them in their own writings, however indirectly.

Autobiographical Samples

My Selection of a Text

Gwin Bristow's "Plantation Trilogy," including her books *Deep Summer* (1937), *The Handsome Road* (1938), and *This Side of Glory* (1940), were popular books among my female peers of early adolescence. The books had been reprinted in paperback in the late 1960s to the early 1970s. I absorbed them each in one to three sittings, often staying up with flashlight under the covers past two in the morning. In looking at them now (particularly *The Handsome Road*) I am intrigued by what about them so captured me at that age—a child not especially drawn to the study of history in school, reading historical fiction into the early mornings. I know there was a sense within me of something magical, hidden, contradictory about the state of Louisiana where I had grown up, though more particularly about southern Louisiana (where I had not lived until adulthood), and that this sense was, in part, instilled by these books.

The Handsome Road tells a story of Civil War Louisiana, mostly from the perspective of a young white woman who was "poor white trash," but also, at times, from the perspective of a wealthy white plantation-owning woman. The genre is similar to the romanticized historical fiction of *Gone With the Wind* (1936). My questions as I initially approached the rereading of this text were around the ways race, class, and gender were constructed. Why would this text be most appealing (at least in the late 1960s to the early 1970s) to young, most likely white, female readers, and to me in particular? What historical sense of place did it achieve for me? How did I situate myself within it ideologically? How did my reading support and/or shape my conceptions of race, class, and gender formation and difference at the time?

There are some other questions of interest to me about this book, which I cannot answer at this time, but which I raise for rhetorical purposes. Why was the book popular enough to go into fourteen printings up through 1973, yet never critically reviewed again after the first few years of publication? The first paperback came out in 1949. By 1969 it was only in its fifth printing. But by 1973 it was in its fourteenth printing. The cover art and blurbs on the 1969–73 paperbacks are clearly aimed at a romance-reading audience. But the book reviews in the late thirties from reputable sources are favorable and treat the book as serious adult reading.

The Handsome Road: *Romance and "Class Consciousness"*

The book opens with a verse entitled "Plantation Song,"

> "Nigger pick de cotton, nigger tote de load,
> Nigger build de levee foh de ribber to smash,
> Nigger nebber walk up de handsome road,
> But I radder be a nigger dan po' white trash!"

which the poor white protagonist, Corrie May, later overhears the slaves singing at a plantation where she has gotten temporary work. This along with numerous other references to slave class condescension toward poor whites sets the tone for the antagonistic way racial difference, from the perspective of the poor white protagonist, is represented through most of the text. At the same time, this situation inspires a kind of "class-consciousness" in Corrie May that enables her to resist fulfilling some of the expectations for a young person of her gender and social class. But, aside from what Corrie May regards as condescending, African Americans in this novel display little agency, and they receive little sympathy.

Throughout most of the book, Bristow maintains a tension in the character of Corrie May between acceptance of the "status quo" for gender and class relations and angry rejection of both. Challenges to interpersonal race relations occur only briefly when Corrie May is under the care of an African-American family in their home as she gives birth to an "illegitimate" son. Interestingly, she names her son after the father of this family.

Bristow condemns slavery in the overt sense, but covertly romanticizes it—leaving out any graphic depictions of abuses at the hands of whites, in fact portraying slave lives as mostly pleasant, but doing so from a distance with no reference to an interior life. On the other hand, graphic depictions of life for poor whites are plentiful. She also frequently romanticizes traditional gender roles and the lives of the "elite" through her uses of language but at the same time seems determined to expose the social construction of such "common wisdom."

It is a contradictory book in much the same manner, perhaps, as particular modern romances are contradictory in their simultaneous challenges to and affirmations of traditional femininity (Radway 1983). As will be demonstrated in what follows, Corrie May steps outside the bounds of traditional femininity and of social class divisions on occasions, at the same time those traditions are left substantially unchallenged. Such contradictions explain to me part of my attraction to it. Growing up in a small north Louisiana town in the Baptist "Bible Belt" with parents who were liberal democrats and non-Christian (at the time), I felt myself to be politically and emotionally in a highly contradictory place (in many senses of the term "place") as a female adolescent. As I reread the book (after nearly twenty years) I found myself engrossed in it all over again—like a fourteen-year-old (Corrie

May is also fourteen in the novel)—at the same time I clearly recognized the style of the writing to be largely predictable and cliched, much like a romance novel.

Now as I reread an essay by Cora Kaplan, *"The Thorn Birds:* Fiction, Fantasy, Femininity," from her book *Sea Changes: Culture and Feminism,*[2] I am struck by the similarity of her adolescent experience in reading *Gone With the Wind* to my own experience with Bristow's books.

> Like many readers of this early blockbuster romance I read it in one bout, too engaged with the story to eat or to sleep. I was a fast reader, but it must have taken me two days; no skipping here for the romance takes up most of the text. My compulsion was observed for the book itself was not approved of; pro-Southern and unashamedly racist, as well as without literary merit in my parents' eyes, it brought together a reactionary political narrative with a reactionary emotional one. I finished the book late in the night and the ending left me in despair and near hysteria. (Kaplan 1987, 117–18)

While Bristow's book was, perhaps, not as politically reactionary as *Gone With the Wind* in the sense that it went farther in challenging the plantation system of the Old South, and my parents did not disapprove my reading it, I did "inhale" the book, and I did react emotionally to it at age fourteen, crying at times for both Corrie May and the wealthy plantation "belle" Ann Sheramy.

A mystique around the old plantation homes was also evoked for me (by then I had visited some of them). These homes embodied the polar opposites of good and evil for me—good in that they were, I thought, romantic and beautiful; evil in that I knew, but probably repressed the knowledge, that people had been held there as slaves and were tortured. I must confess an awe that I still feel, but an awe felt through the undeniable awareness of what those places symbolize. As a graduate student in Louisiana, I had occasion to experience and explore these feelings in the very concrete situation of "house-sitting" one of these homes, Como Plantation, that sits next to the Mississippi River, isolated by four miles of dirt road that dead-ends at the house. Some nights were terrifying.

Como had a particular history for me (which is how I connected for the house-sitting request). I first visited that house fifteen years earlier when it was functioning as a commune for a group of young families and couples. Another monument to/of repression is located near there—Angola, the Louisiana state penitentiary. Rumor had it that Como was the first stop after escape from Angola. (It was the closest property.) The next nearest (and only) home was one mile down the dirt road, and there were no phones at either place. I was advised to leave keys in the car so as to less likely be disturbed. This I did. The "big house" at Como Plantation was a turn-of-the-century structure, built then because the original house had burned to the ground. Nevertheless, it was all there—out there. The place maintained a situation of near-slavery with the "new" house (built just over one hundred years ago) by minting its own currency, running the only businesses in the area, and accepting only the money minted there. As I reread Bristow today, I cannot do other than read her through Morrison, and, of course, through my older self within this and other experiences, as well as my reconstructed adolescent self. Morrison, in *Beloved*, describes aptly what I believe I felt there:

> I was talking about time. It's so hard for me to believe in it. Some things go. Pass on. Some things just stay. I used to think it was my rememory. You know. Some things you forget. Other things you never do. But it's not. Places, places are still there. If a house burns down, it's gone, but the place—the picture of it—stays, and not just in my rememory, but out there, in the world. . . . Where I was before I came here, that place is real. It's never going away. Even if the whole farm . . . dies. The picture is still there and what's more, if you go there—you who never was there—if you go there and stand in the place where it was, it will happen again; it will be there for you, waiting for you. (1987, 35–36)

For Kaplan, rather than an attraction to Southern place born from personal experience, the strength of her attraction to *Gone With the Wind* (henceforth, *GWTW*) lay in its romance and nostalgic embrace of "traditional femininity [that] could be lived in an unashamed way." It was a reaction, in part, to fifties female adolescence and, in part, a form of resistance in a household where the trappings of fifties femininity were disapproved but so was censorship. The way, in Kaplan's estimation, that book spoke to her, as well as to women in general, is worth repeating in full here because I believe her interpretation is relevant for *The Handsome Road*, and for me as well.

> For me personally it was a resonant and painful text, for I was engaged in a long and bitter struggle with my father in these years, for my autonomy, for his love and approval. But it spoke I think to a much wider audience of American women readers for whom the pre-Civil War South did serve as a sort of pre-capitalist site of family romance, a mythical moment of settled traditional social relations that the Civil War destroyed forever. . . . As a parable of Southern history and as a romantic narrative with incestuous overtones it is history and fantasy spoken from the position of the women. It remains so today. (1987, 119)

Rereading *The Handsome Road* as an adult has, I believe, evoked from me what Toni Morrison calls rememory—a sense of having been struck by a glimmering of recollection, of something that has happened but has since been long lost to consciousness. Rememory that occurs through my reading Bristow now calls up questions for me, about myself and my relations to others after I had reached fourteen years of age—questions that have, however, in some way sprung from my vision now of that fourteen-year-old and what happened, what was felt, in her life between then and now. In the context of my current literary and theoretical readings, no doubt Bristow's book has come to mean more and to mean other than it did. Likewise, Kaplan writes of a kind of revisionary repetition of her experience of *GWTW* twenty-five years later with the novel and the television miniseries *The Thorn Birds*. (I, too, watched the entire miniseries on television. I did not know any men who did.) It was through her adult reading of another romance that Kaplan was able to reread her younger self reading GWTW. She writes,

> Like *Gone With the Wind*, but with significant differences, *The Thorn Birds* pursues an interesting occasionally radical interrogation of sexual difference inside a reactionary set of myths about history. (1987, 134)

Like romance novels more generally, as mentioned earlier, each of these texts invite the woman reader to explore limited reversals of traditional femininity and masculinity, all the while, ultimately at least, attempting to bring her back into the fold of traditional female roles. The heroine may resist fulfilling traditional role expectations only to be "conquered" as "Mr. Right" finally arrives (and then, perhaps, he dies!). Here is a sample from *The Handsome Road:*

> Denis came down the hall. He looked tall and splendid, and Ann called herself a fool to hesitate before the chance of the most enviable marriage on the river. As he met her at the foot of the staircase he impulsively swept her into his arms. After a moment Ann drew back a little. She looked up at him, feeling a sensation of pleasure at the nearness of his physical beauty. Denis did not say anything. He stood with one hand on her shoulder and his other arm around her waist, smiling down at her so urgently that Ann felt herself yielding as though his ardor were a command she had no power to disobey, and as Denis drew her to him again she put her own arms around him and pressed his lips down to hers. (1938, 53)

And I loved it. Why?! Such analysis almost frightens me. As Barbara Johnson wrote: "Literature is not only a thwarted investigator but also an incorrigible perpetrator of the problem of sexuality" (1980, 23). Similarly (and to repeat), for Kaplan (who is not Southern), "the deep South and its fake aristocracy, imitation feudalism (which Mitchell both deplores and celebrates) was an imaginary historic site where traditional femininity could be lived in an unashamed way" (1987, 118).

Jessica Benjamin's psychoanalytic theorizing in her book *The Bonds of Love: Psychoanalysis, Feminism, and the Problem of Domination* (1988) is, in my case, illuminating. According to Benjamin, for girls (as for boys) "the father becomes the image of liberation from maternal power . . . the one who recognizes and embodies desire" (100). He is the first "ideal love" in households where certain traditional gender roles are maintained, that is, where the mother's agency is devalued in comparison to the father's. He "seemingly embodies the agency and desire one lacks in oneself" (100). He is "the way into the world" (103).

In such families, the dual desire of the child for separation and identification results in a split whereby the child "assign[s] the contradictory strivings to different parents" (104). This then can result in the devaluation of the mother and the idealization of the father which, for girls, who must necessarily identify with their mothers, presents a particularly difficult dilemma in their struggles for independence. The attraction for women to romance novels is explained by Benjamin as follows:

> In the most common fantasy of ideal love, the one so frequently found in mass-market romances, a woman can only unleash her desire in the hands of a man whom she imagines to be more powerful, who does not depend upon her for his strength. Such a man, who desires but does not need her, satisfies the element missing from *both* mother and father, the ability to survive attack and still be there. In this sense the ideal lover actually provides a dual solution, containment *and* excitement, the holding environment and the road to freedom—the joint features of both the ideal mother and father. (120, emphasis in original)

As I mentioned previously, rereading Bristow induces for me both memory and "rememory" (that sudden, startling, and shadowy "remembrance" of forgotten collective events or thoughts) and, in the context of what Benjamin writes, that memory/rememory takes me to early relationships to my father and to boys. While a full reconstruction of my earlier reading self through Bristow's book is necessarily lacking, the rereading of such a previously read novel provokes memories of long-forgotten events, perhaps even remembering myself remembering, much like the smell of my grandmother's house did. I do remember feeling driven to please my father, to value school as he did, to be a "good girl."

Second grade: I was a new student in Cypress Springs Elementary School. The boy who was class clown did not care that other boys were terrified of and eschewed girls—he loved them. I was new, so I was his next target. He sent a note during class to me, surreptitiously, a love letter. Thrill and mortification. He was outrageous freedom. He said anything at all to the teacher, and still, usually, charmed her. I, on the other hand, was outrageously confined (shy, tentative) by "goodness." I would not acknowledge him. I corrected his spelling and sent the note back. I was my father's daughter.

Memory/rememory: Good girl gone bad. My older sister sneaked out of the house one night to meet her boyfriend. Her empty room was discovered, and I was awakened, questioned, and pleaded with never to do the same, to which I responded, "I would never do that." The very next night: (romance and pain) sneaking out at night together, my sister and I were betrayed by the dog, who led our father to the place of our liaison with our boyfriends. (Damn this small town!) Pounding on the door he yelled, "Give me what's mine!" (My father's daughter.) I remember laughing through fear. A year or so after this event my older sister would follow this guy to Mississippi, only to return home after a few weeks with a bruised face. My boyfriend broke my heart by sleeping with other girls and with emotional distance. I broke up exclaiming, "I never, ever want to see you again!" (Twenty-five years later we are still friends.) Coming to understand this ownership idea has been difficult for me. Do I belong to my father? Do I belong to my partners? Do my partners belong to me? What about friends? Students? What is owed and what is due? It is all *rememory* in that it conjures for me a collective sense of women, perhaps especially Southern women, reading and acting out the romance . . . generations of frustrated and frustrating women and men trapped in a ridiculous drama.

Like *GWTW*, *The Handsome Road* ends with the heroine (Corrie May) and the other primary female character (Ann) "tragically" without husbands or lovers. But unlike Scarlet in *GWTW*, this is not a punishment for "bad behavior"—at least not as explicitly. Still, both women do end up in the presumably much needed care of men—their sons.

Legends and place

Rich descriptions of the natural beauty of south Louisiana in terms of foliage, sunsets, water, smells (which, even in 1938 let alone 1859 to 1865, must have been phenomenal compared to the ravaged and poisoned Louisiana of today) are sprinkled throughout the book. Any mention of the sensuality of natural place—especially in terms of smell—has always captivated my imagination. Interestingly, these descriptions are primarily found in conjunction with scenes of the plantation "big house." For example, Bristow writes of gardenias in the breeze and vetiver sachets for Ann's clothes—two of my favorite scents to this day. It could be argued that this is a strategy for impressing upon the reader the starkness and injustice of the black and poor-white situation by way of pointing out the discrepancies between the two physical environments. Not likely! As I recall, for me at fourteen, such a strategy only served to romanticize the plantation homes to the extent that I found myself hoping they and their inhabitants could go on forever unscathed. I even imagined myself eventually owning one of those homes and becoming a writer—probably of romantic historical fiction. In what follows, I read the text as I see it now.

At the heart of *The Handsome Road* lies Corrie May's determination to both survive and to get beyond living for the mere survival that marks her social class in this poor-white antebellum community just north of New Orleans. Outside town, along the river road, is the stark contrast of the wealthy plantation homes that house the "Southern Gentlemen" who were raised to exploit land and people—especially black people, poor people, and women—with the utmost "courtesy" and "reserve."

> "You'll read the Latin poets, especially Catullus," [the young 'gentleman's' cynical aunt] went on, "and you'll be fond of Byron, and you'll treat every lady as if she were in danger of breaking in two, and say the Army of North Virginia was the greatest bunch of fighting men God Almighty ever let get together on this earth." "I never saw it," said Denis [Ann's son]; rather wistfully. "My dear child, do you think that matters? That's the ultimate test of your type Denis—living by legends you don't know anything about." (1938, 262)

Living by legends. Legends of the "Southern Lady," the plantation myths, of bitterness and blame for Southern defeat (those "damned Yankee Carpetbaggers") survived for me in forms that I could neither recognize nor face at fourteen, but which leapt from the pages for me as I reread and remembered reading. Yet, given the incongruence of my parents' and my own political views with the local and southern majority, I surely considered myself immune, rational, compassionate. I marvel at the strength of history, "real" history rather than mere legend, of hegemony, of place, and, simultaneously, I marvel at the possibility for and incidence of resistance.

Here is that mythical "Southern Lady," "Southern Belle," that "steel magnolia":

> Ann could see herself merging from girlhood into the great lady of the plantation legend. She could do it, not everybody could. A great lady was music and moonshine, but she was also hard as steel. She was too frail to put on her own shoes and stockings but she bore ten children quietly; she had never an idea in her lovely head but she could make a hundred not necessarily congenial guests coalesce into a pleasant unit; she must always be sent upstairs to rest before the ordeal of getting dressed for a ball but she could dance till sunrise once she got there; she turned faint at the sight of blood from a cut finger but she could ride to hounds and be in at the kill. (90–91)

Bristow assures us that, for Ann, this was the natural order. Ann's position could be read through Benjamin's psychoanalytic theory of domination (1988). Such a reaction to difference as exhibited by wealthy white planters can be justified by them only as they see their separation from the "others" as complete. This, however, calls up a contradiction for them in that they require recognition from those others—recognition of their existence as masters, superiors—which creates a dependency that exposes as illusion their absolute separation. Cruelty functions as an attempt to assert and reinforce separation, independence, dominance, and has the effect of reifying those ideas. Indeed, when it comes to social class—"old money," "cultural capital," "poor white trash"—Bristow seems to recognize the illusions of naturalness to social class relations (excluding where such relations involve race) and employs strategies to point this out.

Corrie May is confused at how the wealthy resolve their exploitative cruelty toward the poor with their ethic of tenderness and gentility at home.

For all her glimpses of rich people at Ardeith, she had never made it clear in her mind how they could be so ineffably cruel and at the same time so very kind. There was a woman in Rattletrap Square [Corrie May's neighborhood] whose husband had been killed in a fall from a scaffolding, and she had been turned into the street with four children because she could not pay her rent to the St. Clairs, and yet the very next day Mr. Bertram St. Clair came to dinner at Ardeith with his mother, and he was so attentive to the old lady that he might have been held up as a model of devotion. It was all very puzzling. (111)

Many other examples of this phenomenon are scattered throughout the book, making clear the notion that the wealthy assumed their station in life above poor and black in order to be, perhaps, divinely ordained—natural—and thus justifying a double (or even triple) standard of ethics. Legends survive through double-binds, through contradiction repressed, through the "illiterate imagination" (Harris 1989), in short, through a kind of stupidity.

Ann (Corrie May's employer at the time) and Corrie May each think the other is stupid, and, of course, somewhere they are both right. Ann falls for the "low profile" Corrie May assumes when she is working around the plantation.

She's a funny little thing, Ann thought with irrelevant amusement. So quiet; she doesn't seem to notice very much. Very likely she's a bit stupid. I suppose she's had a hard life, but then she's used to it. People like that don't expect much in the world. (1938, 90)

Then, when Ann asked Corrie May to teach her how to knit in order to support the "war effort,"

Corrie May set about giving her a lesson. In about thirty minutes she was so exasperated she had difficulty keeping her temper. She had never in all her born days seen anybody so stupid as Ann. Those dainty white fingers of hers seemed utterly unable to perform any task at all, even one so simple as throwing thread over a needle. . . . And what was worse, she didn't seem to know how to give her attention to what she was doing. In the middle of an explanation she looked out of

147

the window and said how pretty the moon was as it came up. (108–109)

Both Corrie May and Ann are unable to recognize forms of intelligence in one another—they both assume a natural stupidity in the other. This is exposed by Bristow as she repeatedly points out the differing perceptions.

Corrie May gets involved with a carpetbagger after the war, and she discusses with him why these people—the deposed master class, now poorer than he is—still carry themselves with superiority. She explains to him in her way the notions of cultural capital and the belief by the wealthy in manifest destiny—what she later calls "that magnificent confidence of birth" (285).

> Corrie May hesitated, but she remembered that everybody was equal now and she could say what she pleased, so she continued, "Mr. Gilday, you ain't really going to get at them people till you hit them in the place where they keep a little private contract with their private God that they're better than other folks. They got education and manners and I ain't saying them things ain't fine to have, I wish I had some, but them Larnes and Sheramys and their sort, they honestly think the reason they're like that and you and me ain't is that the Lord God made them out of a different kind of dust from us. It ain't never been in the back side of their mind that if you and me had been started off like them the day we were born we'd be elegant as them now." (183)

Ann, struggling to pay Corrie May's carpetbagger the taxes on her plantation after the war, is humiliated by the man and Corrie May when she is short ten dollars out of one hundred ninety-eight owed. Their snide and haughty behavior toward her is bewildering. "Why do they hate me?" she asks. This historical and interpersonal naiveté is not unlike my own experience of racial relations in Ruston, Louisiana. Certain that I was not racist, I could not understand why I sensed hostility from African-American people or why I felt guilt about that. Nor could I understand why I felt shame, a sort of vague personal responsibility, in the face of African-American deference toward me, as in the case when a woman of color who was baby-sitting my sisters and me offered us a biblical justification for the subordination of dark-skinned people. Did she believe this, really? It seemed so. Or was she saying this only for our benefit? Did I want to believe her? Did she read my desire and play to it? And, if so, was her intent kindness or cruelty? I told her that I did not believe it. Did she believe me?

Corrie May wakes up abruptly to some of the material realities and the social construction of social class differences before the Civil War. She watches her mother, who is thirty-five years old but looks twenty years older than that, and registers that picture alongside her image of Ann Sheramy, who would still look "exquisite" in twenty years, and then recalls her subconscious-turned-conscious hearing of her father's front-porch neighborhood rantings.

> Then, all of a sudden, she heard some of the words Pa had been shooting off as she came down the alley. She had hardly heard them then, she had only felt mad that Pa talked all the time instead of doing a job of work. But they must have gone into her ears and stuck in her head, for now she heard them. In the whole South, seven million white people owning all the slaves. So—if you counted out the slaveowners' families—six million white people who owned no slaves. Six million white people who owned nothing at all. She was not so stupid as not to know that those who owned slaves owned everything else. The first sign of a man's rise in the world was his buying himself a nigger. "Jesus," said Corrie May aloud. (11)

Examples of Corrie May's awarenesses of social class privilege and difference are numerous throughout the book, even including a passage where she notices how much easier it is for a rich couple to make amends after an argument than for a poor couple (because the rich can get away from each other, buy each other consolation gifts, and not have to perform hard labor while angry). Still, race is ever pitted against class in this novel, with the persistent insistence even that slave women were better off than poor white women.

> The mulatto girl Bertha, Napoleon's wife, who expected a baby about the same time as Ann, was appointed for the honor of wet-nursing

the heir; she was moved from the quarters to a room in the big house and coddled with as many luxuries as the mistress. Corrie may thought if it were herself she would have felt like a milch-cow being petted for the parish fair, but Bertha, a smart young woman of elegant speech and manners, put on a multitude of airs. . . . She thought of the slave-women at Ardeith, carefully tended during their pregnancies because a little Negro was worth a hundred dollars the day it was born. (80–81)

Even though it is mentioned that Bertha is mulatto, the reader is apparently not supposed to wonder what this means (assuming the reader's mind-set as a naive fourteen-year-old). Or, if she does know what it means, what the conditions were under which it came about. While Bristow graphically depicts the mob beating of Corrie May for publicly expressing her sentiments about the poor white man being conscripted to fight the rich white man's war (who was not required to fight) in order to insure their respective economic statuses—that is, poor white man "worse off than the slave"—she never mentions the beatings, murders, and rapes suffered by black slaves who did not have the option to just quit their jobs. (This is not to say that it was, in perhaps most cases, much of an option for poor whites, only that there was no such option for slaves, and no legal protection.)

Although Bristow states at the outset that she is writing this from the perspective of the poor whites because most other literature on the antebellum South is either from the perspective of rich white or slave black, I find these kinds of omissions and distortions notable given the presence, albeit somewhat muted, of challenges to the social order in terms of social class. It is difficult to imagine why the black story remains so marginal, in spite of available information on the subject, unless Bristow is so absolutely "other" to black people (a reasonable speculation for 1938 Louisiana) that they are almost nonexistent for her—Ralph Ellison's "invisible" people. Indeed, although Bristow expressed awareness of her privileging of the poor-white story over others, a story of the wealthy white emerges through Corrie May's relations to them. The same cannot be said for her relations to African-American people in the novel. Whether or not Bristow employed a conscious strategy for racial representation, her manner of representation demonstrates a very real distance—an exoticising—of black from white that permeated (and permeates) white consciousness.

Clearly the amount and accuracy of primary sources about the interior lives of slaves was (and is) sorely lacking compared to the multitudes of diaries, journals, newspaper accounts of whites from the same period. According to Elizabeth Fox-Genovese, many of the slave narratives in existence were dictated to white interviewers who either had difficulty with "dialect" or simply censored what they heard, or both (1988, 33). Thus, the slave narratives that possibly were available to Bristow may have presented a skewed image of the lives of slaves. Also, she was writing from the perspective of women, and to find primary sources from black women is apparently even more difficult than from black men. Fox-Genovese says, "Few slave women wrote journals, diaries, and letters. As a group, they did not enjoy even the precarious access to the world of published writings enjoyed by white women and former slave men" (33). Still, it is doubtful that there was much, if any, more material available by or about poor white women. The character of Corrie May was technically illiterate. Indeed, the New Orleans woman who inspired Bristow to create this character and this book could not write her own name. (Bristow worked as a journalist for the *Times Picayune* in New Orleans where she discovered the model for her novel in the obituaries [Bristow 1941].)

After-Words, After-Thoughts: Autobiography and Cultural Studies

In rereading I can begin to reconstruct an adolescent girl who read this book (twenty-six years ago) through locating some of her ignorance—as Shoshana Felman writes, the sites of her "resistance to knowledge" (1987, 80). I was not prepared, as a southern teenaged girl, to relinquish a belief in the romance of the South. Though this novel provided some sense of the inequities and contradictions, it did so without seriously challenging the ahistoricism of Southern romance. Given the mythic characterization of white Southern women as "steel magnolias" which, like myth generally, bears some relation to real people, points of departure from myth and from cliche were few for my adolescent reading as I remember it. Notions of race were as enshrouded in a shimmery vagueness in my rereading of the book as they are for my memories of specific relations to race at fourteen. I sense that race was a kind of undercurrent that beckoned my attention at the same time it was foreboding. It was exoticised, in much the manner it seems to be for Bristow.

I do not presume to be setting forth some direct cause and effect between my adolescent reading of this novel and what or who I became or was. The value of this rereading and rewriting for me is more in its suggestion of the possibility of reconstructing a place (historically, psychologically, geographically) through which I might examine my present relations to others, to myself, to "place"—relations that have a direct bearing on my teaching and notions of knowledge. It has raised for me issues around desire, guilt, privilege, and domination—issues that never cease to concern me in the classroom, in my relations to my students. Indeed, the whole of this study is one outgrowth of my rereading as I initially reread Bristow before I embarked upon this project. As Morrison and Ellison demonstrate, the process Morrison has called rememory is difficult and even painful, but necessary for avoiding existential death. To be existentially dead—caught in the fictional register of identity formation?—is to be in no position to learn/teach. It is to be stupid.

In doing work such as this, one is *doing* a form of cultural studies. One is also employing a fundamental approach to cultural studies more generally and, in this case, ultimately applying it to problems of pedagogy in teacher education. As Richard Johnson writes in "What is Cultural Studies Anyway?":

> the problems [for approaches which focus on "lived culture"] is how to grasp the more *concrete* and *private* moments of cultural circulation. . . . Of course, students of culture have access to private forms through their own experiences and social worlds. This is a continuous resource, the more so if it is consciously specified and if its relativity is recognised. Indeed, a cultural self-criticism of this kind is *the* indispensable condition for avoiding the more grossly ideological forms of cultural study. (1986–87, 69, emphasis in original)

The work of autobiography, as with (and along with) literary reading, is necessarily intertextual and intersubjective.

In arguing the need for a "theory of subjectivity" (63) for cultural studies that takes seriously "the notion of a discursive self-production of subjects, especially in the form of histories and memories" (69), Johnson is also stressing the significance of "readers in texts; readers in society" (65). Moving between readers in texts and readers in societies involves, for Johnson, an intertextual and an interdiscursive competence.

> In disciplinary terms we move from a ground usually covered by liter-
> ary approaches to one more familiar to historical or sociological
> competences, but the common new element here is the ability to han-
> dle a mass of co-existing determinations, operating at many different
> levels. . . . In everyday life, textual materials are complex, multiple,
> overlapping, co-existent, juxtaposed, in a word, "inter-textual." If we
> use a more agile category like discourse, indicating *elements* that cut
> across different texts, we can say that all readings are also "inter-dis-
> cursive." (66–67, emphasis in original)

Autobiography as cultural studies—roughly, studies of the means and ends of self-representation—operates by raising and dynamically responding to the following question: To what extent does a person's constructions of self through narratives about her or his life and reading of texts (especially, here, literary texts) produce new relations and orientations to "culture," and to what extent do these constructions re-produce certain relations and orientations within culture(s)? The self as problematic, intersubjective and perpetual process and project invites us to learn and to nurture a "cross-cultural imagination" or "literacy of the imagination" (Harris 1989).

Student Autobiographies

The course I taught in which the following autobiographical work was done involved theoretical readings for the first half of the semester that loosely centered around sociology and history or education. After some whole-class lecture and discussion each class period, students worked together in small groups of five to six where they were to deal with issues raised in the readings and discussions, often arguing with one another, getting to know one another a bit more intimately than the larger group (about thirty-five students) allowed. The last portion of each class involved whole-class discussions again in which spokespersons from each group would share their group's ideas with the rest of the class. Occasionally, instead of beginning with my lecture, class would begin with presentations on readings by students individually to the entire class in which the student discussed the assigned reading and brought in at least one relevant outside reading. During the latter portion of class, I circulated among the groups, not always getting to each group, where I listened, offered suggestions, and participated in discussions. For the second half of the semester we began reading literary autobiographical writings by Maya Angelou and Annie Dillard. Along with these readings students were to do brief interactive (with the texts) autobiographical writings over three general themes that they selected, in part, from a list of possible themes. At this time, group work involved sharing their concerns and ideas about the readings and writings, receiving critique from their group members if they so chose. Finally, students were required to choose one of their writings and share it (in part or whole) with the entire class. Clearly, such an assignment was frightening for many students at first. I attempted to relieve their sense of vulnerability in a number of ways: first, autobiography was broadly defined to include a number of possible forms such as poetry and autobiographical fiction; second, there were ground rules for the class regarding confidentiality and judgmentalism; third, I began by sharing some of my own work and periodically did so throughout.

In this class, students did receive grades for their autobiographical work. That work was judged, however, primarily on whether or not assignments were done and "attended to"—that is, I asked the question, "Does she or he seem engaged with it?" Something as simple as length of writing can begin to tell me of at least one sort of engagement. But that is clearly insufficient. Was the tone of the writing glib? Did they rely on cliches? Even if they did rely on cliches, sometimes that was not an indication of insincerity or nonengagement so much as inexperience and repression. For this reason and others I was glad that I had waited, as planned, until midterm to begin this work, a time after which I was better acquainted with my students than at the beginning, and had gained a sense of certain kinds of boundaries. Indeed, it seemed that many apparent limits were overcome—students went "beyond themselves"—with the autobiographical work. Beyond this it is not easy to articulate specific criteria for judging, but I can say that I found very few students who did not get taken in by the project, some enjoying it in spite of themselves. I say "in spite of themselves" because there was resistance to the idea at first. I know this from signals given in class, but also, more concretely, from voluntary, anonymous written evaluations given to me at the end of the semester. Still, the greatest difficulty I have encountered so far is in finding ways to discourage students from producing something like "Muzak" versions of their lives. Though several of them did succumb to this in at least some of their writings, clearly, many of them avoided it. All names are pseudonyms.

Love and the pedagogical imperative

Trish wrote about her reading self. She loves to read and learned to love it from, she believes, one high school teacher in particular. She writes:

> *English had always been my favorite subject and I was doing quite well in his class. He made the literature seem lively and interesting and his rapid fire discussions went over well. One day he asked me to stay after class. He said that he had liked my report on* The Catcher in the Rye *and asked if I would be interested in doing some extra reading. Until that time I had only read what was assigned in school. In fact, I remember thinking that he was offering me extra credit. But what he offered was a stack of his own books that he'd had when he was my age. I didn't think I would be interested in all this extra "work." But, always anxious to please the teacher, I took them.*
>
> *A strange thing happened as I delved into Harper Lee and Mark Twain—I constantly thought about Mr. Thibodaux. What did he think about the story and the characters? Had he laughed and cried at the same*

places I had? I hungrily read everything he suggested in preparation for the "big moment." That was once a week when after class he would fold his hands, tilt his head, and ask, "Well, what have you been reading?" I had developed a huge crush on him and this was the only time he spoke to me on any kind of personal level. Needless to say, I lived for this moment and was always sure to be well-prepared for the ensuing discussion.

Trish then writes of returning to her high school after four years—four years of "reading like a madman"—to visit Mr. Thibodaux. She was shocked at the profound difference in her earlier impression of his physical appearance and what she saw now. The prior obsession, she now realized, was based in a kind of transference love (though she did not call it that) that her high school self was unable to disentangle from feelings of romantic love. Indeed, as discussed earlier, such love cannot be viewed as in clear distinction.

In private conversation Trish told me that she still falls in love with good teachers, though not with the same illusions. She was concerned about this and asked me if I understood—if I did the same thing. She was particularly distressed over the fact that this most often occurred for her with her male professors. Reminding her that probably most of her professors are male, I did offer the suggestion that she give this some thought by writing about it in the context of her current readings for the class.

Indeed, in her next writing she asked herself the question, "Why are most of the teachers I loved male?" She writes:

I don't think that most of the teachers I've "loved" have to do with that kind of crush/romantic love as in the case of Mr. Thibodaux. I think that in my feelings for the good teachers there is a determinable amount of respect. But in trying to find examples of really good female teachers I can only come up with two . . .

She then initiates an exploration of her different expectations for male and female teachers with a quote from Annie Dillard's *An American Childhood*: "They [boys] had been learning self-control. We [girls] had failed to develop any selves worth controlling" (1987, 91). Trish writes:

What a scary, scary passage. Does it really start that young? How many things must be undone to expose this conditioning that is begun so early? Is it possible? I know that this feeling exists in me and I reject it to the point of meanness. This is not a good solution! So what can be done about something that is so prevalent in our society?

Trish's "meanness" is, she discovers, in that her female teachers must work much harder than her male ones to win her respect. Female teachers that she had liked as an elementary and high school student had been likable because they were "sweet," but all too often this sweetness was manifested in low expectations for students, particularly girl students. Trish, it seems, resented this as she grew older and discovered her own mind. That resentment resulted in prejudgment for female teachers, and a kind of subconscious requirement that they work harder now, for atonement. Trish is deeply disturbed at her own complicity in patriarchy implicit in this attitude.

I am not suggesting that Trish necessarily came to some deep psychoanalytic understanding of notions of desire and transference, nor that this is necessary. However, I do think it possible that she has been set on a trajectory of discovery of sorts with her new way of reading both texts and herself. My own interpretation of her writing and our conversations is that Trish has encountered a "surprise of otherness" in her recognition, through reading and writing, of some of the cultural foundations of her reactions to male and female teachers, as well as the possibilities for departures from cultural "scripts." She has encountered the significance of otherness not only in her reconstructed perceptions of Mr. Thibodaux and her female teachers, but also within herself.

Transformations and difference (past and present)

At the end of the semester Donna writes:

I've tried and tried to title this writing, but I just can't find one that is suitable. So, I'll just jump straight into what I want to say. This is a combination of me, Donna, trying to explain both to myself, and to you, my teacher, what this class has taught me about "otherness," and how it has changed my vision of myself as a teacher.

I have always been a very prejudiced person, although that is something I never would have admitted, perhaps even to myself, before this course. My prejudices, although they include racial ones, are certainly not exclusive to them. I have grown up with the belief that I was better than "others." "Others," in my life, were people who looked different, acted different, wore the wrong kind of clothes, drove the wrong car, held the wrong job, had a poor ACT score, a bad perm, a strange accent. The list is almost endless. I would certainly never have voiced my opinion; that would be tacky, cruel. No one that knows me would ever accuse me of being unkind, stuck-up, or even prejudiced. But in my mind, these feelings lived.

When I made the decision to teach, I began to see the potential conflict between my desire to be a good teacher, and the intolerance I felt. In this day and age, such biases are easy to justify, but I wasn't fooling myself. This wasn't right, and it wasn't the person I wanted to be. How could I be a good teacher, change students' lives, be someone they respected and hold on to these beliefs. I couldn't.

The early readings in this course began to give me something concrete to think about. These things made sense! As a teacher, it was important for me to alienate no one, to show no favoritism or bias. All of these children deserve the best education I could give them, and I knew that "hiding" my biases would not work.

Maya Angelou's I Know Why the Caged Bird Sings *spoke more directly to my heart. This was a wonderful, brilliant child. A child with questions and feelings very much like I would have, had I been in her situation. But society has not treated me like it treated her, like it treats so many children. That was the only real difference between me and Maya. I read Maya Angelou's book twice; I couldn't get enough of it the first time. I began to look at the people around me differently. Why did I have so little patience with others? Wasn't that why I wanted to teach, to bring something to someone who did not have it before? How could I expect everyone to be like me? They could easily ask the same of me!*

I also have had to face up to why this class was so difficult for me to engage in throughout the semester. This was trying ground for me to cover, new ground. These were questions I had not yet resolved for myself, and I was hesitant to deal with these things in a large group of people. However, this class has gone a long way toward helping me to answer my questions about myself. I have begun to resolve the inner struggles that my desire to teach has generated. I'm glad that I have chosen a future and a profession that is making me into a better person, a person that I can respect.

Note: This is the last essay that I actually wrote. Although it deals with a topic for the first week, in my mind and heart, it ties together what this semester has meant to me.

This writing brings to the fore a number of questions. Was Donna writing just what she thought I wanted to hear? Of course, I have no way of answering this definitively, but given the intensity of her writing, to answer it in the affirmative seems an act of distrust. She was a very quiet student, as her writing might indicate, and I had no idea until this time that she felt as she did about the class. Her grades had all been high as well—there was no need to attempt to please me on that account.

More importantly for me is the question of how or if this differs, in result or in apparent goal, from those "human relations" approaches to, and models for, multicultural education that I have criticized and wished to go beyond. Certainly, it seems clear that Donna has experienced a change in attitude toward cultural differences—the primary stated goal of human relations multicultural education. But I want to make the argument that her change has been toward the very idea of difference, and that this constitutes, for Donna, a new way of reading—of reading, similar to Trish, for the surprise of otherness.

This can be discussed by looking at a few key sentences in her writing. Some of her statements are problematic in the context of this project. For example she writes, "But society has not treated me like it treated her, like it treats so many children. That was the *only real difference* between me and Maya." This urge to collapse very real differences between herself and Angelou may be a necessary step in her construction of herself, much like Pinar advises with his thermostatic notion of an "architecture of the self." We build it according to what needs attending for the moment. Plans can always be changed later. Donna's sense of herself as utterly separate from "others" may need addressing before concerns about "fusion." That she will stop with this construction is in no way implied by her particular reading.

Then, in the same paragraph, she writes: "How could I expect every-one to be like me? They could easily ask the same of me!" Is this merely a "human relations" gesture? I think it probably encompasses that but I do not think it is merely that. Through certain literary works it is possible for students to learn a new way to read . . . a new assem-blage is constructed. That is more than mere change in attitude as it is typically framed in the goals of "human relations" multicultural curric-ula—curricula which sought to generate harmony across difference without ever interrogating the historical and cultural sources of gen-uine conflict. Finally, I *am* talking about "human relations." But not about the sort of human relations that ignores larger contexts of the social, the cultural, the historical, and the political. My students, in these examples, I believe, are discovering the ways in which culture is made at both macro and micro levels. They discover the fallacy of viewing tradition as a monocultural commodity rather than a dynamic transformation produced by encounters between and among cultures. We are produced not only by what we "do to" others, but also by their responses to that and vice versa. To read "tradition" as "common cul-ture" pure and simple becomes absurd from this perspective.

It is not my intention to set these examples up as some sort of "proof" that ideas in this writing have been tested and found to "work." I believe that, in fact, these examples are contradictory enough to point to the need for further study (in terms of possible uses) in the context of teacher education classrooms. For these same reasons, although I have many more examples of student autobiographical writing, I will not include more writings here. To do so would only serve to dominate the chapter with embryonic "data," and to undermine my purpose in writing it.

Conclusion

The self-reflective writing that has been done in and for my classroom and by myself, as well as the type of student and teacher work I am sug-gesting in this study through theoretical explorations, calls for a reconceptualization of multicultural teacher education and curriculum.

This reconceptualization involves attending to the historical and current development of cultural studies as well as to the politics of identity. Literary and autobiographical studies glimpsed through a cultural studies lens are interdisciplinary and intertextual. The approaches I envision and have attempted to describe operate through awareness of what Geertz has called "blurred genres" (1983)—another phrase for studies being approached within and through other disciplines, and particularly through "textual" approaches. Students reading and writing about literature in conversation with self, through awareness of social and cultural theory as well as the philosophical and psychological underpinnings of such theory, are learning to read difference and otherness at a depth not typically available to students of multicultural teacher education. This is, indeed, a tall order. I am not suggesting that the job could be completed in this class from which I have drawn examples. To the contrary, it is just a beginning. Such an intellectual approach requires *not* a course or two on multicultural education and self-reflective reading and writing, but an entire curriculum of study in which educational studies are envisioned as inherently multicultural, personal, and, in significant senses, as a "liberal arts discipline" (Beyer, Feinberg, Whitson, and Pagano 1991). The particular way in which Beyer, et al. frame their conception of educational studies as liberal art is indeed interdisciplinary and one which echoes many of the concerns of cultural studies.

6

Translating Chaos

BOUNDARIES, BORDERS, CONNECTIONS, CONCLUSION

You are born at the same time with a lot of other people, all mixed up with them, like trying to, having to, move your arms and legs with strings only the same strings are hitched to all the other arms and legs and the others all trying and they dont know why either except that the strings are all in one another's way like five or six people all trying to make a rug on the same loom only each one wants to weave his own pattern into the rug.[1]
—William Faulkner, *Absalom, Absalom!*

THIS PASSAGE seems an apt description of the way problems get served up in daily living, and those that I have attempted to explicate in this writing are no exception. One might feel that such an image is echoed in poststructuralist theorizing whereby nothing is ever certain, stable, unified, or closed, but always in some sort of turbulent process. Particular and engaging literature presents itself to us somewhere inbetween daily life and theory. Yet at the same time, "theory is here often the straight man whose precarious rectitude and hidden visibility, passion, and pathos are precisely what literature has somehow already foreseen" (Johnson, B. 1980, xii).

If literature is comedian to theory's straight man, then poststructuralist theory must surely be a kind of literature to other kinds of theory.
Through poststructuralist theory we have been taught the ways in which
deconstruction can avoid some of the constraints of dialectical thinking,
and how it is possible to let go of some of the certainty we have sometimes so desperately, so obsessively, and at times so oppressively, clawed
after. Poststructuralist theorizing seems to be looking into (or listening
into?) creating an environment in which living can be sufficiently playful,
loving, adventurous, and so on. But this theorizing sometimes *appears* to
want to skip over the step of obliterating overt physically/materially
manifested oppressions—to pretend that they have already been taken
care of, and that we can move on now. At worst this theorizing is oblivious to its own conservatism, caught in denial and repression (that it also
denies), presenting no serious challenge to whatever is.

Varieties of structuralist materialist theorizing, on the other hand,
hold another set of potential traps and contradictions. The primacy of
the material that supports human need—its availability, control, and
movement—is a fundamental presupposition of materialist theories. As
such these theories are generally and logically first and foremost social
class-based theories. What this has meant historically is that class concerns have been privileged over others such as race and gender,
"because, we are told, it [class] is more fundamental than any other
interests or forms of social power" (Young 1990, 4).

As I have labored to explain, any discourse which polarizes, posing the
one as good and the other as evil, or one as primary and the other as
merely secondary, is suspect in terms of its own capacity for violence
and totalization. Although I make efforts to avoid this, my discourse is
no exception. Most differences, however, are matters of degree and not
matters of distinction. The very difficulty of avoiding such polarization
can be appreciated, and degrees of failure forgiven, once we glimpse the
dazzling complexity of human (and other) existence and relationships.
Hence, I must say, materialism as an informing system must be taken
into account. Indeed, contradictions among "the ruling class" over issues
of culture in the present configuration are material (structural) as well as
psychosocial or discursive. For example, with well known demographic
trends toward a "majority minority," manifestations of a fear of falling

from the center (fears of, primarily, white male academics) are often operating in direct opposition to corporate movements in their visions of future marketing and employment needs. In this respect it could be that "capitalism, out of self-interest, [will] facilitate our entrance into a new stage of race relations" (Martinez 1991, 130). However, it is difficult to predict what shape this "stage" may take given the still strongly entrenched underlying ideological construction of white supremacy.

This is where educational institutions might be able to provide critical intervention. However, the sort of intervention I envision—one which seriously interrogates the politics of identity and culture—is difficult to impossible if the discourse of white supremacy is allowed to remain invisible and extra-topical in academic debates. This discourse plays itself out in many particular ways and forms: popular culture and media, policies of the state, institutional practices, academic theories, and so on. All of these discursive forms contribute to the psychosocial climate that produces subjectivities and notions of identity. Such a discursive field also takes particular shapes and textures according to the particular cultural ecologies in which it is functioning. Educational interventions that do not take such particularities into account amount to a kind of *intellectual tourism* (Roman, cited in McCarthy 1988b)— tourism that is unable to directly, materially challenge dominant ideologies of white supremacy and patriarchy.

Intellectual tourism results when scholars refuse to figure particular cultural forms, subjectivities, and agencies into their theoretical formulations and, instead, subsume all of these under singular, totalizing social theories, such as with liberal and radical theories of social class, as well as conservative and neoconservative theories of cultural deprivation (McCarthy 1988b). Within such a paradigm "Third World" subjects become objects as do marginalized groups in the "First World." Likewise, one can learn to read like a tourist (as do students within such systems)—a learned illiteracy, a block functioning—reading oneself into everything, one-way translation that reads others only through the lenses of a singularly conceptualized, dominant culture, reading that literally precedes itself in exotic fantasizing. I mean by "precedes itself" that it is prefigured; (re)interpretation is unnecessary. It is the type of reading Mariah and her husband did of Lucy (in Kincaid's *Lucy*) whereby Lucy's pedagogical attitude was interpreted as her way of expressing to them what a "hard life" she (and "her people") had had.

My own efforts here and in my classroom are to expose that "will to ignore" that leads to learned illiteracy so that a new condition for reading is possible. This is reading that discloses to the reader her or his own desire to ignore, to repress, to seek "bottom line" closure everywhere. Once again, it is reading that "encounters and propagates the surprise of otherness" (Johnson, B. 1987, 15). Reading for the surprise of otherness, like identity formation across Taubman's three registers, is always reading via someone/something else. This someone else is not only, in part, other than the reader, it is also, in part, other than the author. It is translation without a master.

Like the impossibility of fully escaping the *metaphysics of presence* (Derrida 1976), this goal or outcome is unrealizable in any absolute sense. The process of working toward this is what is significant. However, process does not imply method. As Johnson explains, "No methodology can be relied on to generate surprise. On the contrary, it is usually surprise that engenders methodology" (15). This "literacy of the imagination" (Harris 1989) is a literacy that does not answer to the notion of an "excellence" (in education) that exists above and apart from notions of "equity," two ideas that are often pitted against one another in popular rhetoric about school reform. It is, I believe, a move toward the same literacy that Whitson refers to when he writes, "the point is that literacy requires the dialogue that bigotry prevents, so that the bigot is and must be a bad reader" (1988, 294). One cannot "see" (or hear) the familiar until it is made strange. Western culture is best understood in the context of studies of "other" cultures, including the ways in which these cultures encounter and transform one another. And this reading of the world necessarily takes place in the context of, and in relation to, reading the self.

Cultural Studies Toward a Politics of Identity

Literature and Identity

"Listening to the non-synchronous voices from the periphery" (McCarthy 1988b, 17), Faulkner's gaze might become Ellison's (musical) hearing. Theoretical voices from the periphery are still grossly underrepresented, even in the literature of cultural studies. Even when theory written by the marginalized has been included it has been highly derivative of Anglo or European theory. For example, no one would guess from Stuart Hall's earlier work that he is an African-Caribbean immigrant to England. More often, voices from the periphery that generate "otic" theories—theories of listening—are literary voices. The gazing "ocular" "abstractions of western sociology . . . that negate the specific histories of third world people" (18) and other marginalized groups demand a response that only a "literature of resistance" (18) and "translation as an act of resistance" (Niranjana 1992, 84) can provide. McCarthy offers an eloquent plea:

> I argue for a genuine, interdisciplinary encounter between third world and New World literature and popular cultural forms and Old World derived sociology of education as the basis of an alternative radical discourse that would render audible the heterogeneous voices of oppressed raced, classed, and gendered third world subjects. (18)

The power of such literature becomes most evident when measured next to the stridency and shrillness of conservative attacks against it—attacks intended to conserve what is thought to be Western cultural tradition as embodied in canonical literature. When cultural studies scholars insist to traditionalists ("canonizers") that they do not wish to eliminate canonical works, traditionalist arguments proceed through a different tack. What was the ahistorical becomes the antihistorical.

Literature becomes canonized presumably because it is great as proven, in part, by "the test of time." It is great and enduring, so the argument often goes, because it contains universal truths—verities. But "universal truths" or values are hard to pin down because the contexts in which these texts are read is ever-shifting. To assert the existence of universal truths is to assert a kind of final interpretation—an ahistorical stance. Currently, in critiques of multiculturalism, traditionalists are frequently going further than just to say the "great works" should always be taught. Now they are more insistent about the way they should be taught. Particular readings of canonical texts that take into consideration social/historical contexts that may include uncovering racism or sexism, for example, are under attack for "reducing literature to 'ideology'" (Berube 1991, 37). Complaints about "ideological" readings of texts are often really complaints about historical readings. It is in this sense that what was the ahistorical becomes now the antihistorical. So who, Berube asks, is being reductive?

In these debates attacks against "political correctness" are often veiled attacks against cultural studies as well as exhibitions of profound insecurities over *national identity*. "Multiculturalists," cultural studies scholars, the so-called politically correct, do need to pay attention to these expressions of fear and desire. The Left academics, some of whom are scholars of the politics of culture, who are accused of this intolerance, have been steadily losing advocates because of a failure to acknowledge particular problems of *individual identity*—perhaps especially those problems of the autobiographical register (in spite of the fact the ostensible arguments are over *national* identity). People who might wish to be social activists but feel demoralized, in need of emotional support at a time when there are few social rewards for activism, have been accused of being self-indulgent. Consequently, support groups with names like "adult children" or "recovering addicts" are getting the commitments from people who might otherwise be peace or civil rights activists, for example (Herman 1991, 42–46). "No one, of course, should have to make the impossible choice between personal and social change" (46).

The problems with this move to embrace psychological health to the exclusion of commitment to social health are obvious. Once again, identity is "lived" as if it operates out of a single register, only this way it is the autobiographical rather than the communal. The fallacy of such a unidimensional approach to identity is evident, for example, in the ways in which some psychological practitioners have historically supported politically repressive goals through such moves as offering "incontrovertible evidence of homosexual psychopathology, and design[ing] propaganda to efficiently destroy radical organizations" (46). Clearly, when identity problems are relinquished to such practitioners the social and political problems are multiplied. As Herman suggests, progressive change is predicated on rejection of "the dualism between internal and external transformation" (46). A politics of culture and identity approached through literature can perhaps provide a reparation.

The anxiety over "eternal truths" in canonical literature could be read as a search for a kind of consolation. Italo Calvino wrote in *The Uses of Literature* of the fallacy of seeing literature merely as

> an assortment of eternal human sentiments, as the truth of a human language that politics tends to overlook. . . . Behind this way of thinking is the notion of a set of established values that literature is responsible for preserving, the classical and immobile idea of literature as the depository of a given truth. If it agrees to take on this role, literature confines itself to a function of consolation, preservation, and regression. (cited in Goodman 1991, 124)

Calvino offers an alternative way to view literature. It becomes most useful

> when it gives a voice to whatever is without a voice, when it gives a name to what as yet has no name, especially to what the language of politics excludes or attempts to exclude. (124)

Voices from the periphery, to be heard, require a cultural studies of listening, an "otic" theory. For me, good literature is written work which engages readers by appealing to similarities at the same time it provides glimpses at and avenues of escape into difference, marginality, otherness. To do this, literature itself has to listen. Literature, then, often begins in the mundane but takes a "line of flight," in Deleuze's sense of that phrase, out of the mundane. It is a frontier of sorts (Deleuze and Parnet 1987, 36–51).

Autobiography and Identity

But what about the "ocular" character of autobiography whereby a "specular structure" presents itself the moment a writer "declares himself the subject of his own understanding" (de Man, cited in Smith 1988, 103)? The purely specular image of self reflecting (upon) self is a frozen image, trapped in the infinite regress of a hall of mirrors. How is this reconciled with the call for theorizing that undermines "the gaze" and that promotes justice and democracy rather than narcissism? Self gazing upon self gives way to listening as soon as that self recognizes its own division, its *relational* necessity, its very definition in dynamic relationality, and its (non-neurotic) instability. It is difficult to see something that always moves away, but movement is essential for creating sound, for hearing. The instability I prefer is also related to biology. Though life seems to "seek" equilibrium, it is the movement of disequilibrium that enables it to adapt . . . in fact, to become stable. A paradox. With autobiography that asserts itself only in relation (in relation to margins) and through disequilibrium, particular, regional and repressed histories can be recovered and rearticulated as they are with literature of the margins.

The self that is not in mastery of itself (or of anyone) recognizes its own division, its own disequilibrium, instability, and *impurity* (and is, paradoxically, a more stable self). That division is, in part, about race. As Deleuze and Guattari remind us:

> there is no race but inferior, minoritarian, there is no dominant race, a race is not defined by its purity but rather by the impurity conferred upon it by a system of domination. Bastard and mixed blood are the true names of race. (1990, 12)

(Susie Phipps embodies this story.) With regard to the "impurity" that defines race, the pure, unified, raceless, undivided, gazing self is a *paranoid* self. Recall what Paul Smith writes about paranoia: "the 'subject' thus endows the external world with what it takes to be its own worst tendencies and qualities" (1988, 95). The "subject" projects its own pessimistic inner concoctions onto the world it "sees." Theories of the visual are analogous to the paranoid—a kind of "metaparanoia" (97). As in Faulkner's Rosa and Ellison's Brotherhood, and as Halpin points out (1990), those ocular theories (theorists) presume to see all but believe that they themselves cannot be seen and indeed work to cover

over their own visibility. "Purity" is invisible, "natural," raceless. It "sees" but cannot be seen. Within this "metaparanoia," "The division of the 'subject' (the division it makes and the division it is) is thus *hidden* for the purposes of a mastery" (Smith 1988, 97, emphasis added).

That (stable) instability that is "self," that is *not* neurotic, not divided *against* itself, can be "seen" through a new conception of a nonvisual approach to theorizing. Literature and autobiography are vital to that project. Because the exhilaration and significance of reading/writing and writing/reading literature lie somewhere between the tentative naming of oneself and plunging into difference, I encourage students and teachers to think about directing their writing toward such "discoveries" (inventions?).

The stories we create about ourselves are, in part, what determine our perceptions of ourselves and, as such, influence what we become to ourselves and others. The self is constructed by the writing, but not as a static, final self. Rather, it becomes a self-in-motion, reading and writing in such a way as to recognize the fictional, communal, and autobiographical registers of identity as interpenetrating and deconstructing one another, or in dialectical tension, depending on the situation. Yet, the larger questions for this study have become: What is a better way to come to "know" difference, both cultural and individual? How can we work to understand both cultural and individual difference both intra- and intersubjectively? And how can that work be woven into curricula?

Many argue that the best way to understand cultural difference is through immersion. But even were this a possible, practical, approach for (multicultural) teacher education, it still requires of the participant a suspension of resistance to difference that living within a different culture does not necessarily insure. Certain literary works can provide a kind of "practical" immersion, while autobiographical work done alongside literary readings can serve as a medium for suspending resistance to difference by placing the self positively within that difference, as in the case, for example, of my student Donna. At the same time, readings from the cultural studies traditions can provide the tools for deepening such an approach, for thinking through social, cultural and literary theories as they inform intertextual readings of literary works of different times and cultures, and thereby remind us of the truly multi-cultural encounters that create and sustain us.

Final Remarks

It is clear that British cultural studies holds no monopoly on those ideas that inspired and sustained it, such as the ideas of studies that challenge disciplinary boundaries and that dare to work from the academic margins in order to avoid appropriation by the dominant political order(s). Many disciplines of the traditional liberal arts and social sciences are increasingly viewing themselves as actors through such scholarly approaches—for example, in anthropology, Geertz proclaims the necessary acknowledgment of "blurred genres" (1983); in philosophy, poststructuralists proclaim the primacy of literary texts as philosophical texts (e.g., Guattari 1990); literature, philosophy, and autobiography are bound together for the purpose of psychotherapy (White and Epston 1990); and these same elements are employed in the service of historiography (Portelli 1991). Nevertheless, "cultural studies" as a movement that provided much of the early labor for these others must be acknowledged and their struggles remembered lest the difficulties be unnecessarily repeated. Its history and labors have as yet informed the work of multicultural education scholars only marginally. It is as though we have believed that our teacher education students cannot be troubled with such a heavy intellectual burden. Such a belief is not justified by my own experiences through approaches described in this study—approaches that have now been shared with both undergraduate and graduate students of education.

However, a difficulty remains for me with the autobiographical work over which there must never be complacency. The fact that many students may respond to autobiographical assignments with such an intensity as to indicate that they want, indeed are hungry, to tell their tales does not absolve me of the responsibility of questioning my rights to ask for them and my ways of asking for them. People often want what is not in their best interests. The question of whether or not to proceed this way comes back to me always as an uneasy one at best. With Grumet, I feel that:

> if my work permits the teachers I work with to examine their own work with a seeing that is more inclusive, that surveys an ever widening surround, that is a search I would gladly join. But if my work certifies me as an agent of the state to peer into what is hidden from public view, if it is my look that discovers and appraises, then I might as well approach the classroom with bloodhound as well as briefcase, and they ought to demand to see my warrant before they let me in. (1991, 71)

No, it is not for us to peer into private lives as agents of the state. It is for us to "shift attention away from assertions of power to the instrument through which that power is exercised" (Morrison 1994, 12). In her Nobel acceptance speech Toni Morrison recalls a woman: old, blind, and known to be wildly wise. The woman is visited by some young people who hope to test her reputation of wisdom. They tell her they hold a bird in their hands, and ask her if it is living or dead. After a very long pause, and some giggles from the young people, the woman replies, "I don't know. I don't know whether the bird you are holding is dead or alive, but what I do know is that it is in your hands. It is in your hands" (11). The instrument through which the power is exercised is the bird-in-hand, "the bundle of life sacrificed" (12) or saved. Language is the bird, and the responsibility for its use is "in your hands," whoever you are—teacher, student, reader, writer. Finally, I cannot justify what I do beyond what *I* see (or think I see), and have attempted to describe and explain here, as a growth of *love*. And I write this word (love) in hopes that it will not be read as a regressively sentimental idea, full of sweetness and harmony, but rather in the context of the ways it has been written and thought in earlier chapters.

And finally (again! can we not have more than one finale?!), it is *love* that brings together literature, marginality, and curriculum. As Daignault pointed out (1989) to me (and as I later found for myself with excursions through English language etymological dictionaries), the Latin infinitive for religion, *religere*, means to reread and to care.

(*Negligere* is its Latin opposite and means negligence). *Curare*, different but similar in sound and spelling to *currere*, also means to care. *Cultus* (culture) means care; worship. And love is related in my own text to both care and to religion (in the sense of spirituality) as well as desire. "Leave is the offspring of yet another Indo-European root, *leubh-* 'to care, to desire; to love'" (Partridge 1982, 189). And this leaves us with crisis—Greek, *krisis* (a separating, decision, discrimination); Latin, *discrimen* (interval, intervening space, turning point, difference, risk). The risk of loving—caring, deciding, discriminating, and finally leaving (in any number of senses)—is common to the educational enterprise and to literature. And it is living in the midst of this risk (crisis) that marks the margins in all its layers. I leave you with this. Now it is in your hands. Because, "look where your hands are. Now" (Morrison 1992, 229). *What knowledges best enable us to minimize violence to ourselves, one another, and the nonhuman world?* That is the curriculum question.

> Implicit in all this is the notion that a truly creative alchemical response to crisis and conflict and deprivation—a response that engages with formidable myth—may well come from the other side of a centralised or dominant civilisation, from extremities, from apparently irrelevant imaginations and resources. The complacencies of centralised, ruling powers—where language tends sometimes to become a tool for hypocrisies and false clarities—begin to wear thin at the deep margins of being within a multi-levelled quest for the natures of value and spirit. That quest becomes more and more imperative within endangered environments and species and communities.
>
> Inner confidence, inner hope, may gain unpredictable momentum at the edges of capacity, *through* fissures of capacity in which the scope and the potentials of buried traditions re-vision themselves. (Harris 1989, 30, emphasis in original)

Notes

1. Introduction

1. In fairness to Jane Gallop, she includes work by two feminists in the field of education, or curriculum theory to be more exact—Madeleine Grumet and Jo Ann Pagano. But to my knowledge, this is a first.

Perhaps it is not surprising, however, to find that feminist scholars *do* seem to be reaching toward their feminist sisters and brothers in education who have written books about feminist pedagogy. At least I am finding this to be the case in communications through electronic lists. Frequently the names Patti Lather, Jennifer Gore, Carmen Luke, and a few others are suggested as readings for a list called "feminist pedagogy," subscribed to by women's studies scholars and those in other disciplines who identify themselves as feminists.

2. In using the term "marginalized" at this point I am explicitly referring to marginality that is determined by race and/or colonialism, and sometimes gender as a compounding determinant. Marginality in the larger sense will be discussed much more fully in the third chapter, and my emphasis on race, colonialism, and gender will be explained.

3. See Donna Harraway's "The promises of monsters: A regenerative politics for inappropriate/d others," 1992. I share Harraway's concerns about the politics of representation, both in human-human interactions as well as in the larger ecology of human–non-human coconstruction. She writes:

> Some actors, for example specific human ones, can try to reduce other actors
> to resources—to mere ground and matrix for their action; but such a move is

contestable, not the necessary relation of "human nature" to the rest of the world. Other actors, human and unhuman, regularly resist reductionisms. The powers of domination do fail sometimes in their projects to pin other actors down; people can work to enhance the relevant failure rates. Social nature is the nexus I have called artifactual nature. The human "defenders of the forest" do not and have not lived in a garden; it is from a knot in the always historical and heterogeneous nexus of social nature that they articulate their claims. Or perhaps, it is within such a nexus that I and people like me narrate a possible politics of articulation rather than representation. (311)

And earlier:

Science becomes the myth not of what escapes agency and responsibility in a realm above the fray, but rather of accountability and responsibility for translations and solidarities linking the cacophonous visions and visionary voices that characterize the knowledges of the marked bodies of history. (299)

2. Multiculturalism into Cultural Studies

1. My own position, listed in 1991 at the University of Illinois at Chicago, was described in the *Chronicle of Higher Education* as a position in "curriculum and cultural studies." I have no reason to believe that anyone there connected that title to the tradition of British cultural studies.

2. I want to emphasize that the term *canonical* is being used loosely here. Anyone can create a canon or a concrete curriculum. The *concept* of canon is an essentialist one. That is the point.

3. It is interesting here to note which periodicals had top circulations in 1995. According to the *Information Please Almanac, Reader's Digest* topped the list at over 16 million; *TV Guide* is second with just over 14 million; *National Geographic* sold over 9 million; *Better Homes & Gardens* sold 7.6 million; the closest next competitors range from over 5 to over 3 million in the following (descending) order: *Good Housekeeping, Ladies Home Journal, Family Circle, Woman's Day, McCall's, Time, People Weekly, National Enquirer, Playboy, Sports Illustrated, Redbook, Prevention, Newsweek.*

3. Theory and Difference

1. While the notion of "choosing the margins" will be further explained and developed in later paragraphs and chapters, it is important to be clear that choosing does not mean appropriating another's culture, or claiming superior knowledge of a social position in which one has no personal stake or experience.

2. The term *currere of marginality* is apt in the context of this writing in another sense: curriculum theory as a field of study is itself marginalized in academia generally. And this marginalization is at one and the same time oppressive (low funding, negligence, threats of obliteration, etc.) and enlightening (there is relative freedom to explore multiple perspectives due to a sort of "benign neglect" within power structures, there exists the possibility of a version of "double consciousness" within the academy). As such, curriculum theory is a place of encounters between and translations among different local knowledges—a process which itself constitutes the generation of new knowledges. It is not simply derivative of other fields. This idea places curriculum theory, in many senses, in a similar situation to cultural studies. We either become artists and scholars or we die—fulfilling "the role of the artist and the role of curriculum theorists as seers of the intersections of humanity and things condemned by vocation to marginality" (C. McCarthy, personal communication, May 1990).

3. Probably few would deny that literature has value far beyond that of pleasure and escape (not that those values are not inextricably linked to the others), but in many of the social sciences, including my own field of curriculum theory, and even the natural sciences (e.g., Serres 1982b; Harraway 1992; and Hayles 1990), the potential power of literature to inform those fields has only recently begun to be articulated. In teacher education "whole language" and "literature-based instruction" are widely known and fairly frequently in practice now in elementary schools. Both approaches make use of literature for all areas of the curriculum. My elementary education students in the social studies methods class found literature to be a vital part of their curriculum of marginality. It often filled the gaps and connected isolated blocks between textbooks for different subjects, and between textbooks and other more primary representations of the same subjects where no other materials could.

4. I use the term *antiviolent* rather than the usual *nonviolent* because I believe that communication, translation, knowledge, education, and therefore curriculum are inescapably "violent" to degrees. Hence, a perfectly nonviolent translation or curriculum is impossible.

4. Translating Curriculum with Literature and Cultural Studies

1. A "literature of the margins" could be compared to what Deleuze and Guattari call a "minor literature": "We might as well say that minor no longer designates specific literatures but the revolutionary conditions for every literature within the heart of what is called great (or established) literature" (1990, 61).

5. Autobiographical Heirs (Airs)

1. Autobiographical writing, writing and theorizing about autobiography in education, and other related notions such as "teacher lore" (Schubert 1991), "voices of teachers" (Aoki 1990), "narrative dialogue" (Witherell and Noddings 1991), "reflective practice" (Schon 1983, 1991), and "teacher stories" (Pagano 1990, 1991) have been a part of curriculum discourses over the last several years (e.g., also, Abbs 1974; Ayers 1989; Grumet 1980, 1988a, 1988b; Miller 1990; Pagano 1991; Pinar 1980, 1981, 1988, in press; Pinar and Grumet 1976; Taubman, in press). Many of these projects have been explorations into the uses of autobiography for teacher education and their implications for curriculum praxis. Some have been for the purpose of self-exploration for curriculum theorists and teacher educators. Some also investigate and generate theorizing about autobiography itself.

2. I want to thank Leslie Roman for pointing out the Kaplan chapter to me, recognizing its similarity to my story.

6. Translating Chaos

1. This was one of the very few speaking parts for Faulkner's Judith.

References

Abbs, P. 1974. *Autobiography in education*. London: Heinemann Educational Books.

Althusser, L. 1971. *Lenin and philosophy*. New York: Monthly Review Press.

Angelou, M. 1969. *I know why the caged bird sings*. New York: Random House.

Aoki, T. 1990. Voices of teaching. Monograph. Program for Quality Teaching, 1, British Columbia Teachers' Federation.

Asante, M. K. 1987. *The afrocentric idea*. Philadelphia: Temple University Press.

———. 1988. *Afrocentricity*. Philadelphia: Temple University Press.

Ayers, W. 1989. *The good preschool teacher: Six teachers reflect on their lives*. New York: Teachers College Press.

Baker, G. 1973. Multicultural training for student teachers. *The Journal of Teacher Education* 24: 306–7.

Baker, H. 1987. To move without moving: An analyis of creativity and commerce in Ralph Ellison's *Trueblood Episode*. In *Speaking for you: The vision of Ralph Ellison*, edited by K. Benston. Washington, D.C.: Howard University Press.

Banks, J. A. 1981. *Multiethnic education: Theory and practice*. Boston: Allyn and Bacon.

———. 1987. *Teaching strategies for ethnic studies*. Boston: Allyn and Bacon.

Banks, J. A., and C. A. M. Banks, eds. 1989. *Multicultural education: Issues and perspectives*. Boston: Allyn and Bacon.

Bateson, G. 1972. *Steps to an ecology of mind*. New York: Ballantine.

Benjamin. J. 1988. *The bonds of love: Psychoanalysis, feminism, and the problem of domination*. New York: Pantheon Books.

Benstock, S., ed. 1988. *The private self: Theory and practice of women's autobiographical writings*. Chapel Hill: University of North Carolina Press.

Bennett, W. J. 1984. *To reclaim a legacy: A report on the humanities in higher education*. Washington, D. C.: National Endowment for the Humanities.

———. 1988. *Our children and our country: Improving America's schools and affirming the common culture*. New York: Simon and Schuster.

Berube, M. 1991. *Village Voice*, 18 June, 31–39.

Beyer, L., W. Feinberg, A. Whitson, and J. Pagano. 1991. *Preparing teachers as professionals: The role of educational studies and other liberal disciplines*. New York: Teachers College Press.

Bloom, A. 1987. *The closing of the American mind*. New York: Simon & Schuster.

Boyers, R. 1985. *Atrocity and amnesia: The political novel since 1945*. New York: Oxford University Press.

Bristow, G. 1937. *Deep summer*. New York: Thomas Y. Crowell.

———. 1938. *The handsome road*. New York: Thomas Y. Crowell.

———. 1940. *This side of glory*. New York: Thomas Y. Crowell.

———. 1941. Gwen Bristow: a self-portrait. In the Louisiana Collection, Hill Memorial Library. Louisiana State University.

Buckingham, D. 1984. The whites of their eyes: A case study in responses to educational television. In *Education for a multicultural society*, edited by M. Straker-Welds. London: Bell and Hyman.

Bullivant, B. 1981. *The pluralist dilemma in education*. Sydney: Allen and Unwin.

Cash, W. J. [1941] 1969. *The mind of the South*. New York: Vintage Books.

Cheney, L. 1988. *Humanities in America*. Washington, D. C.: National Endowment for the Humanities.

———. 1989. Current fashions in scholarship diminish the value of the humanities. *The Chronicle of Higher Education*, 8 February, A40.

Clement, C., and H. Cixous. [1975] 1988. *The newly born woman*. Trans. B. Wing. Minneapolis: University of Minnesota Press.

Cooke, M. G. 1984. *Afro-American literature in the twentieth century: The achievement of intimacy*. New Haven: Yale University Press.

Covi, G. 1990. Jamaica Kincaid and the resistance to canons. In *Out of the kumbla: Caribbean women and literature*, edited by C. Davies and E. Fido. Trenton, NJ: Africa World Press.

References

Cortes, C. 1973. Teaching the Chicano experience. In *Teaching ethnic studies: Concepts and strategies*, edited by J. Banks. Boston: Allyn and Bacon.

Daignault, J., and C. Gauthier. 1981. The indecent curriculum machine: Who's afraid of sisyphe? *Journal of Curriculum Theorizing* 1: 177–96.

Davis, R. C., and R. Schleifer, eds. 1989. *Contemporary literary criticism: Literary and cultural studies*. New York: Longman.

Deleuze, G., and F. Guattari. 1983. *Anti-Oedipus: Capitalism and schizophrenia*. Trans. R. Hurley, M. Seem, and H. R. Lane. Minneapolis: University of Minnesota Press.

———. 1990. What is a minor literature? In *Out there: Marginalization and contemporary cultures*, edited by R. Ferguson, M. Gever, T. T. Minh-ha, and C. West. Cambridge, MA: MIT Press.

Deleuze, G., and C. Parnet. [1977] 1987. *Dialogues*. Trans. H. Tomlinson and B. Habberjam. New York: Columbia University Press.

Derrida, J. 1976. *Of grammatology*. Trans. G. C. Spivak. Baltimore: Johns Hopkins University Press.

———. 1981. *Positions*. Chicago: University of Chicago Press.

———. 1985. *The ear of the other: Otobiography, transference, translation*. Trans. P. Kamuf; and *Otobiographies: The teachings of Nietzsche and the politics of the proper name*. Trans. A. Ronell. Edited by C. V. McDonald. New York: Schocken Books.

Descombes, V. [1979] 1980. *Modern French philosophy*. Trans. L. Scott-Fox and J. M. Harding. Cambridge: Cambridge University Press.

Dillard, A. 1987. *An American childhood*. New York: Harper & Row.

Dominguez, V. R. 1986. *White by definition: Social classification in creole Louisiana*. New Brunswick, NJ: Rutgers University Press.

Donnelly, D. H. 1984. *Radical love: An approach to sexual spirituality*. Minneapolis: Winston Press.

DuBois, W. E. B. [1906] 1969. *The souls of black folk*. New York: Penguin Books.

Education Week. Here they come, ready or not. Vol. V, no. 34, 14 May 1986, 14–37.

Ellison, R. W. 1952. *Invisible Man*. New York: Vintage Books.

———. 1953. *Shadow and act*. New York: Vintage Books.

Faulkner, W. 1936. *Absalom, absalom!* New York: The Modern Library.

Felman, S. 1982. Psychoanalysis and education: Teaching terminable and interminable. *Yale French Studies* 63: 21–44.

———. 1987. *Jacques Lacan and the adventure of insight: Psychoanalysis in contemporary culture*. Cambridge, MA: Harvard University Press.

Felman, S., and D. Laub. 1992. *Testimony: Crises of witnessing in literature, psychoanalysis, and history.* New York: Routledge.

Ferguson, R. 1990. Introduction: Invisible center. In *Out there: Marginalization and contemporary cultures,* edited by R. Ferguson, M. Gever, T. T. Minh-ha, and C. West. Cambridge: MIT Press.

Finn, C. E., D. Ravitch, and R. T. Fancher, eds. 1984. *Against mediocrity: The humanities in America's high schools.* New York: Holmes & Meier.

Finn, C. E., D. Ravitch, and P. H. Roberts, eds. 1985. *Challenges to the humanities.* New York: Holmes & Meier.

Fish, J. 1981. The psychological impact of field work experiences and cognitive dissonance upon attitude change in a human relations program. Unpublished doctoral dissertation, University of Wisconsin-Madison.

Fiumara, C. G. 1990. *The other side of language: A philosophy of listening.* Trans. C. Lambert. New York: Routledge.

Foucault, M. 1988. Technologies of the self. In *Technologies of the Self,* edited by L. H. Martin, H. Gutman, and P. H. Hutton. Amherst, MA: Univ. of Massachusetts Press.

Fox-Genovese, E. 1988. *Within the plantation household: Black and white women of the old South.* Chapel Hill: University of North Carolina Press.

Freire, P. 1970. *Pedagogy of the oppressed.* Trans. M. B. Ramos. New York: The Seabury Press.

———. 1994. *Pedagogy of hope: Reliving pedagogy of the oppressed.* New York: Continuum.

French, M. 1985. *Beyond power: On women, men, and morals.* New York: Ballantine Books.

Fuss, D. 1989. *Essentially speaking: Feminism, nature and difference.* New York: Routledge.

Gallop, J., ed. 1995. *Pedagogy: The Question of Impersonation.* Bloomington: Indiana University Press.

Garcia, E. 1974. Chicano cultural diversity: Implications for competency-based teacher education. In *Multicultural education through competency-based teacher education,* edited by W. Hunter. Washington, D.C.: American Association of Colleges for Teacher Education.

Gates, H. L., ed. 1985, 1986. *"Race," writing and difference.* Chicago: University of Chicago Press.

———. 1987. *Figures in black: Words, signs, and the "racial" self.* New York: Oxford University Press.

References

———. 1988. *The signifying monkey: A theory of Afro-American literary criticism.* New York: Oxford University Press.

Gay, G. 1990. Achieving educational equality through curriculum desegregation. *Phi Delta Kappan* (September): 56–62.

Geertz, C. 1983. Blurred genres: The refiguration of social thought. In *Local knowledge: Further essays in interpretive anthropology,* edited by C. Geertz. New York: Basic Books.

Gibson, M. 1984. Approaches to multicultural education in the United States: Some concepts and assumptions. *Anthropology and Education Quarterly* 15: 94–119.

Giroux, H. A. 1988. *Schooling and the struggle for public life: Critical pedagogy in the modern age.* Minneapolis: The University of Minnesota Press.

———. 1992a. *Border crossings: Cultural workers and the politics of education.* New York: Routledge.

———. 1992b. Resisting difference: Cultural studies and the discourse of critical pedagogy. In *Cultural Studies,* edited by L. Grossberg, C. Nelson, and P. Treichler. New York: Routledge.

———. 1994. Doing cultural studies: Youth and the challenge of pedagogy. *Harvard Educational Review* 64(3): 278–308.

Giroux, H., A. Penna, and W. Pinar, eds. 1981. *Curriculum and instruction.* Berkeley: McCutchan Publishing Corporation.

Glazer, N. and D. Moynihan. 1963. *Beyond the melting pot.* Cambridge, MA: Harvard University Press.

Goldstein, R. 1991. The politics of political correctness. *Village Voice,* 18 June, 39–41.

Gollnick, D. M. 1980. Multicultural education. *Viewpoints in Teaching and Learning* 56: 1–17.

Goodman, M. 1991. PC debates I: The alchemy of bias. *Zeta Magazine* (July/August): 120–25.

Gorra, M. 1995. The autobiographical turn: Reading the new academic autobiography. *Transition* 5(4): 143–53.

Graff, G. 1992. *Beyond the culture wars: How teaching the conflicts can revitalize American education.* New York: W. W. Norton & Company.

———. 1993. The pedagogical turn. Paper presented to the conference for the Midwest Modern Language Association, Minneapolis, MN. November.

Graham, R. 1991. *Reading and writing the self: Autobiography in education and the curriculum.* New York: Teachers College Press.

Gray, R. 1986. *Writing the South: Ideas of an American region.* New York: Cambridge University Press.

Greenblatt, S. J. 1976. Learning to curse: Aspects of linguistic colonialism in the Sixteenth century. In *First images of America,* edited by F. Chiappelli. Berkeley: California University Press.

Greene, M. 1975. *Teacher as stranger.* Belmont, CA: Wadsworth.

———. 1988. *The dialectic of freedom.* New York: Teachers College Press.

Griffin, G. 1992. *Calling: Essays on teaching in the mother tongue.* Pasadena, CA: Trilogy Books.

Grossberg, L., C. Nelson, and P. Treichler, eds. 1992. *Cultural studies.* New York: Routledge.

Grossberg, L. 1995. Cultural studies: What's in a name (one more time). *Taboo* 1 (Spring): 1–37.

Grover, J. Z. 1992. AIDS, keywords, and cultural work. In *Cultural Studies,* edited by Grossberg, Nelson, and Treichler. New York: Routledge.

Grumet, M. 1991. The politics of personal knowledge. In *Stories lives tell: Narrative and dialogue in education,* edited by C. Witherell and N. Noddings. New York: Teachers College Press.

———. 1988a. *Bittermilk: Women and teaching.* Amherst: University of Massachusetts Press.

———. 1988b. Women and teaching: Homeless at home. In *Contemporary curriculum discourses,* edited by W. F. Pinar. Scottsdale, AZ: Gorsuch Scarisbrick.

Guattari, F. 1990. The three ecologies. Paper presented at Louisiana State University, Baton Rouge.

Gunn, J. V. 1982. *Autobiography: Toward a poetics of experience.* Philadelphia: University of Philadelphia Press.

Gusdorf, G. [1956] 1980. Conditions and limits of autobiography. In *Autobiography: Essays theoretical and critical,* edited by J. Olney. Princeton: Princeton University Press.

Gwin, M. 1985. *Black and white women of the old South: The peculiar sisterhood.* Knoxville: University of Tennessee Press.

Hall, S. 1980. Cultural studies and the center. In *Culture, media, language,* edited by S. Hall, D. Hobson, A. Lowe, and P. Willis. London: Hutchinson.

———. 1987. Minimal selves. In *Identity: The real me,* edited by H. Bhabha. London: Institute of Contemporary Arts [ICA Documents].

———. 1990. The emergence of cultural studies and the crisis of the humanities. *October* 53: 11–23.

———. 1992. Cultural studies and its theoretical legacies. In *Cultural studies*, edited by L. Grossberg, C. Nelson, and P. Treichler. New York: Routledge.

Hall, S., D. Hobson, A. Lowe, and P. Willis, eds. 1980. *Culture, media, language*. London: Hutchinson.

Halpin, E. 1990. The ocular and the otic: Theoretical paradigms in Faulkner and Ellsion. Unpublished manuscript.

Harraway, D. 1992. The promises of monsters: A regenerative politics for inappropriate/d others. In *Cultural studies*, edited by Grossberg, Nelson, and Treichler. New York: Routledge.

Harris, W. 1983. *The womb of space: The cross-cultural imagination*. Westport, CT: Greenwood Press.

———. 1989. Literacy and the imagination—a talk. In *The Literate imagination: Essays on the novels of Wilson Harris*, edited by M. Gilkes. London: MacMillan.

Hayles, N. K. 1990. *Chaos bound: Orderly disorder in contemporary literature and science*. Ithaca, NY: Cornell University Press.

Hemenway, R. 1977. *Zora Neale Hurston: A literary biography*. Chicago: University of Illinois Press.

Herman, E. 1991. Liberation politics: Toward a politics of self esteem? *Zeta Magazine* (July/August): 42–46.

Heshusius, L. 1994. Freeing ourselves from objectivity: Managing subjectivity or turning toward a participatory mode of consciousness? *Educational Researcher* (April): 15–22.

Hirsch, E. D. 1987. *Cultural literacy: What every American needs to know*. Boston: Houghton Mifflin.

Hodge, R., and G. Kress. 1988. *Social semiotics*. Ithaca, NY: Cornell University Press.

Hoggart, R. 1958. *The uses of literacy*. London: Penguin.

hooks, b. 1990. *Yearning: Race, gender, and cultural politics*. Boston: South End Press.

———. 1994. *Teaching to transgress: Education as the practice of freedom*. New York: Routledge.

Hurston, Z. N. [1937] 1978. *Their eyes were watching God*. Chicago: University of Illinois Press.

———. [1942] 1984. *Dust tracks on a road: An autobiography*. Chicago: University of Illinois Press.

Jakobson, R. 1959. On linguistic aspects of translation. In *On translation*, edited by R. Brower. Cambridge, MA: Harvard University Press.

Johnson, B. 1980. *The critical difference: Essays in the contemporary rhetoric of reading.* Baltimore: Johns Hopkins University Press.

———. 1987. *A world of difference.* Baltimore: Johns Hopkins University Press.

Johnson, R. 1986–87. What is cultural studies, anyway? *Social Text* 16: 38–80.

Kanpol, B., and P. McLaren, eds. 1995. *Critical multiculturalism: Uncommon voices in a common struggle.* New York: Bergin & Garvey.

Kaplan, C. 1987. *Sea changes: Culture and feminism.* London: Verso.

Kerby, A. P. 1988. The adequacy of self-narration: A hermeneutical approach. *Philosophy and Literature* 12: 232–45.

Kincaid, J. 1978. *At the bottom of the river.* New York: Farrar, Straus and Giroux.

———. 1983. *Annie John.* New York: Farrar, Straus and Giroux.

———. 1988. *A small place.* New York: Farrar, Straus and Giroux.

———. 1990. *Lucy.* New York: Farrar, Straus and Giroux.

Kristeva, J. 1982. *Powers of horror: An essay on abjection.* Trans. L.S. Roudiez. New York: Columbia University Press.

———. 1987. *Tales of love.* New York: Columbia University Press.

Kundera, M. 1981. *The book of laughter and forgetting.* New York: Penguin Books.

———. 1984. *The unbearable lightness of being.* New York: Harper & Row.

Lasch, C. 1984. *The minimal self: Psychic survival in troubled times.* New York: W. W. Norton.

Levinas, E. 1989. *The Levinas reader,* edited by S. Hand. Cambridge, MA: Basil Blackwell.

Lionnet, F. 1989. *Autobiographical voices: Race, gender, self-portraiture.* Ithaca: Cornell University Press.

Lutz, C. A. 1988. *Unnatural emotions: Everyday sentiments on a micronesian atoll & their challenge to Western theory.* Chicago: University of Chicago Press.

Martinez, E. 1991. PC debates II: Willie Horton's gonna get your alma mater. *Zeta Magazine* (July/August): 126–30.

McCarthy, C. 1988a. Rethinking liberal and radical perspectives on racial inequality in schooling: Making the case for nonsynchrony. *Harvard Educational Review* 58: 265–79.

———. 1988b. Slowly, slowly, slowly, the dumb speaks: Third World popular culture and the sociology of the Third World. *Journal of Curriculum Theorizing* 8(2): 7–21.

———. 1990. *Race and curriculum: Social inequality and the theories and politics of differences in contemporary research on schooling.* Philadelphia: Falmer Press.

References

————. 1993. After the canon: Knowledge and ideological representation in the multicultural discourse on curriculum reform. In *Race, identity and representation in education*, edited by C. McCarthy, and W. Crichlow. New York: Routledge.

McCarthy, C., and W. Crichlow, eds. 1993. *Race, identity and representation in education*. New York: Routledge.

McCormick, T. W. 1988. *Theories of reading in dialogue: An interdisciplinary study*. Lanham, MD: University Press of America.

Miller, J. L. 1990. *Creating spaces and finding voices: Teachers collaborating for empowerment*. Albany, NY: SUNY Press.

Mitchell, M. 1936. *Gone with the wind*. New York: Macmillan.

Mitchell-Kernan, C. 1973. Signifying. In *Mother wit from the laughing barrel*, edited by A. Dundes. Englewood Cliffs, NJ: Prentice Hall.

Moreland, R. 1993. "He wants to put his story next to hers": Putting Twain's story next to hers in Morrison's *Beloved. Modern Fiction Studies* 39, 3 & 4: 501–525.

Morrison, T. 1987. *Beloved*. New York: Alfred A. Knopf.

————. 1989. Unspeakable things unspoken: The Afro-American presence in American literature. *Michigan Quarterly Review* (Winter): 1–34.

Morton, D., and M. Zavarzadeh, eds. 1991. *Texts for Change: Theory/pedagogy/politics*. Chicago: University of Illinois Press.

Mull, M., and A. Rucker. 1985. *The history of white people in America*. New York: Perigee.

Murray, D. 1991. *Forked tongues: Speech, writing and representation in North American Indian texts*. Bloomington: Indiana University Press.

Nadel, A. 1988. *Ralph Ellison and the American canon: Invisible criticism*. Iowa City: University of Iowa Press.

Nelson, C., ed. 1986. *Theory in the classroom*. Chicago: University of Illinois Press.

Niranjana, T. 1992. *Siting translation: History, post-structuralism, and the colonial context*. Berkeley: University of California Press.

O'Donovan, O. 1980. *The problem of self-love in St. Augustine*. New Haven: Yale University Press.

Ollman, B. 1986. The meaning of dialectics. *Monthly Review* 38: 42–55.

Olney, J., ed. 1980. *Autobiography: Essays theoretical and critical*. Princeton: Princeton University Press.

Omi, M., and H. Winant. 1986. *Racial formation in the United States: From the 1960s to the 1980s*. New York: Routledge and Kegan Paul.

Otten, T. 1989. *The crime of innocence in the fiction of Toni Morrison.* Columbia, MO: University of Missouri Press.

Pagano, J. 1990. *Exiles and communities: Teaching in the patriarchal wilderness.* New York: SUNY Press.

———. 1991. Moral fictions: The dilemma of theory and practice. In *Stories lives tell: Narrative and dialogue in Education,* edited by C. Witherell and N. Noddings. New York: Teachers College Press.

Partridge, E. 1983. *Origins: A short etymological dictionary of modern English.* New York: Crown Publishers.

Perry, D. 1990. An interview with Jamaica Kincaid. In *Reading black, reading feminist,* edited by H. Gates. New York: Meridian.

Pettigrew, L. E. 1974. Competency-based teacher education: Teacher training for multicultural education. In *Multicultural eduction through competency-based teacher education,* edited by W. Hunter. Washington, D.C., American Association of Colleges of Teacher Education.

Pinar, W. F. 1975. *Currere:* Toward reconceptualization. In *Curriculum theorizing: The reconceptualists,* edited by W. Pinar. Berkeley: MuCutchan.

———, ed. 1988. *Contemporary curriculum discourses.* Scottsdale, Arizona: Gorsuch Scarisbrick.

———. 1991. Curriculum as social psychoanalysis: On the significance of place. In *Curriculum as social psychoanalysis: The significance of place,* edited by J. Kincheloe and W. Pinar. New York: SUNY Press.

———. 1994. Autobiography and an architecture of self. In *Autobiography, politics and sexuality: Essays in curriculum theory 1972–1992,* edited by W. F. Pinar. New York: Peter Lang.

Pinar, W. F., and M. Grumet. 1976. *Toward a poor curriculum.* Dubuque, IA: Kendall/Hunt Publishing Company.

Pinkerton, E. C. 1982. *Word for word.* Essex, CT: Verbatim Books.

Portelli, A. 1991. *The death of Luigi Trastulli and other stories: Form and meaning in oral history.* Albany, NY: SUNY Press.

Rabinow, P., and W. M. Sullivan, eds. 1987. *Interpretive social science, a second look.* Berkeley: University of California Press.

Radway, J. A. 1983. Women read the romance: The interaction of text and context. *Feminist Studies* 9(1): 53–78.

Rajchmann, J. 1991. *Philosophical events: Essays of the 80's.* New York: Columbia University Press.

References

Ravitch, D. 1990. Multiculturalism yes, particularism, no. *The Chronicle of Higher Education* (24 October): A44.

Ravitch, D., and C. E. Finn. 1987. *What do our 17-year-olds know?: A report on the first national assessment of history and literature.* New York: Harper & Row.

Reed, I. 1973. *Mumbo jumbo.* Garden City, NY: Doubleday.

Riesman, D., N. Glazer, and R. Denney. 1969. *The lonely crowd.* New Haven: Yale University Press.

Robbins, T. 1987. An interview with Tom Robbins. In *Alive and writing: Interviews with American authors of the 1980s,* edited by L. McCaffery and S. Gregory. Chicago: University of Illinois Press.

Rooney, E. 1990. Discipline and vanish: Feminism, the resistance to theory and the politics of cultural studies. *Differences* 2: 14–28.

Schneiderman, S., ed. 1980. *Returning to Freud: clinical psychoanalysis in the school of Lacan.* New Haven: Yale University Press.

Schon, D. A., ed. 1991. *The reflective turn: Case studies in and on educational practice.* New York: Teachers College Press.

———. 1983. *The reflective practitioner: How professionals think in action.* New York: Basic Books.

Schubert, W. 1991. Teacher lore: A basis for understanding praxis. In *Stories lives tell: Narrative and dialogue in education,* edited by C. Witherell, and N. Noddings. New York: Teachers College Press.

Selden, R. 1989. *A reader's guide to contemporary literary theory.* Lexington: University Press of Kentucky.

Serres, M. 1982a. *The parasite.* Trans. L. R. Schehr. Baltimore: Johns Hopkins University Press.

———. 1982b. *Hermes: Literature, science, philosophy.* In J. V. Harrari and D. F. Bell, eds. Baltimore: Johns Hopkins University Press.

Sleeter, C. 1991a. Multicultural education as a form of resistance to oppression. Unpublished manuscript.

———, ed. 1991b. *Empowerment through multicultural education.* New York: SUNY Press.

———. 1993. How White Teachers Construct Race. In *Race, identity and representation in education,* edited by C. McCarthy and W. Crichlow. New York: Routledge.

Sleeter, C., and C. Grant. 1987. An analysis of multicultural education in the United States. *Harvard Educational Review* 57: 421–44.

Smith, P. 1988. *Discerning the subject.* Minneapolis: University of Minnesota Press.

Snitow, A. 1987. Death duties: Toni Morrison looks back in sorrow. *VLS* 58: 25–26.

Soble, A. 1990. *The structure of love*. New Haven: Yale University Press.

Spivak, G. C. 1988. Explanation and culture: Marginalia. In her *In other worlds: Essays in cultural politics*. New York: Routledge.

———. 1989. In a word. Interview with Ellen Rooney. *Differences* 1: 124–56.

———. 1993. *Outside in the teaching machine*. New York: Routledge.

Sprinker, M. 1980. Fictions of the self: The end of autobiography. In *Autobiography: Essays theoretical and critical*, edited by J. Olney. Princeton: Princeton University Press.

Starobinski, J. [1976] 1980. The style of autobiography. In *Autobiography: Essays theoretical and critical*, edited by J. Olney. Princeton: Princeton University Press.

Tate, C. 1987. Notes on the invisible women in Ralph Ellison's *Invisible Man*. In *Speaking for you: The vision of Ralph Ellison*, edited by K. Bensten. Washington, D.C.: Howard University Press.

Taubman, P. 1993. Separate identities, separate lives: Diversity in the curriculum. In *Understanding curriculum as a racial text*, edited by W. Pinar and L. Castenell. New York: SUNY Press.

Taylor, M. C. 1987. *Altarity*. Chicago: University of Chicago Press.

Thompson, E. P. [1964] 1978. *The making of the English working class*. London: Penguin.

Turner, G. 1990. *British cultural studies: An introduction*. Cambridge, MA: Unwin Hyman.

Twain, M. [1884] 1985. *Adventures of Huckleberry Finn*. Berkeley: University of California Press.

Viadero, D. 1990. Battle over multicultural education rises in intensity. *Education Week* (28 November): 1, 11–13.

Watkins, B. T. 1989. Scholar's panel calls humanities healthy, assails critics' views. *The Chronicle of Higher Education* (11 January): A1, A11–12, A14, A16–17, A20, A22.

White, M., and D. Epston. 1991. *Narrative means to therapeutic ends*. New York: W. W. Norton & Company.

Whitson, A. 1988. The politics of "non-political" curriculum: Heteroglossia and the discourse of "choice" and "effectiveness." In *Contemporary curriculum discourses*, edited by W. Pinar. Scottsdale, Arizona: Gorsuch Scarisbrick.

References

Williams, R. [1958] 1966. *Culture and society: 1780–1950*. London: Penguin.

———. [1961] 1975. *The long revolution*. London: Penguin.

Winkler, K. J. 1990. Proponents of "multicultural" humanities research call for a critical look at its achievements. *The Chronicle of Higher Education* (28 November): A5, A8–9.

———. 1991. Organization of American historians backs teaching of non-Western culture and diversity in schools. *The Chronicle of Higher Education* (6 February): A5–7.

Witherell, C., and N. Noddings, eds. 1991. *Stories lives tell: Narrative and dialogue in education*. New York: Teachers College Press.

Worton, M., and J. Still, eds. 1990. Introduction. In their *Intertextuality: Theories and Practices*. New York: Manchester University Press.

Wright, R. [1940] 1966. *Native son*. New York: Harper & Row.

Young, R. 1990. *White mythologies*. New York: Routledge.

Index

Index

Crichlow, W., 4
"cross-cultural imagination", 60, 74,
    153
"Crossing the Disciplines: Cultural
    Studies in the 1990s" [conference],
    17
cultural deprivation models and theory,
    12, 59
cultural differences, 34
culturalism, structuralism and, 20
Cultural Literacy (Hirsch), 1, 27
cultural studies, 2, 4
    autobiography and, 151–153
    in Britain, 12–22, 172, 176(n1)
    contemporary ideas of, 16–18
    definition of, 22–27
    multiculturalism into, 11–35
    the self and, 121–131
    toward a politics of identity, 166–167
    translation of curriculum with,
    78–119
Cultural Studies [anthology], 18
"Cultural Studies Now and in the
    Future" [conference, 1991], 17
Culture and Society (Williams), 18
"Culture Wars", 27–35
cultus, 174
curare, 174
currere
    of marginality, 37–48, 66, 73, 89,
    177(n2)
    origin of term, 38
curriculum, translation with literature
    and cultural studies, 78–119
Cypress Springs Elementary School,
    143

Daignault, Jacques, 44, 122, 123, 124,
    173
Davis, Robert Con, 17
dead white males, 34
decentered subject, 33

deconstruction, 33–34, 42–48, 51
Deep Summer (Bristow), 136
Deleuze, G., 9, 53, 169, 170, 177(n1)
de Man, Paul, 108
Derrida, Jacques, 17, 41, 43, 45, 54, 92,
    125
de-territorialization, 59
Dewey, John, 3, 20
dialectics, 42–48
difference, theory and, 37–74
differences, concepts of, 73
Dillard, Annie, 154, 156
Dilthey, 20
discrimen, 174
Donna, student autobiography of,
    157–159, 171
Donnelly, D. H., 64, 66
"double consciousness", 130
Douglass, Frederick, 107
DuBois, W. E. B., 3, 130
Dust Tracks in the Road (Hurston), 56

eco-erosic love, 62, 79
"ecology of mind", 62
Edmonson, Munro, 50
Ellison, Ralph, 5, 40, 51, 59, 73, 74, 80,
    81–84, 89, 90–102, 103–104, 107,
    112, 150, 152, 166–167, 170
eros, 62, 67, 84
    Christian concept of, 64
essentialism(s), 30, 31
    atheoretical, 62
    definition of, 8–9
    essence of, 48–53
    as manifestations of block function-
    ing, 35
Euro-American, as Western, 34
European-Americans, 47, 48

Family Circle, 176(n3)
Fancher, R. T., 33
father love, 65

Index

Index

"The Ocular and the Otic: Theoretical Paradigms in Faulkner and Ellison" (Halpin), 101
O'Donovan, O., 64
Oklahoma Project for Discourse and Theory in 1990, 17
Ollman, Bertel, 42, 45
Olney, James, 124–125, 126
otic theory, of literature, 169

Pagano, Jo Ann, 125–126, 132, 133, 136, 161
Paradise Lost (Milton), 118
paranoia, 170
parental love, 65
pedagogy
  psychoanalysis implication to, 78
  writers on, 4
A People's History of the United States (Zinn), 77
People Weekly, 176(n3)
Perry, Donna, 114, 118
Perse, St.-John, 118
Phipps, Susie, 50, 61
Pinar, William, 1, 38, 39, 47, 99, 130, 133, 134, 159
plantation homes, 139, 145
"Plantation Trilogy" (Bristow), 136
Plato, 64, 65
Playboy, 176(n3)
pluralism, 12
"political correctness", 5, 28
  criticisms of, 32
politics of difference, 33
politics of identity, 33
poor whites, depiction in Southern literature, 138, 145, 146, 150
Portland "baseline essays", for history, 29
postmodern literary style, 115
postmodern self, 130
postmodern subjects, 33

post-positivism, 33
poststructural literary style, 115, 125
prejudice, 34
Prevention, 176(n3)

quotas, 34

race
  depiction in Southern literature, 150–151
  I.Q. and, 34
Race, Representation, Identity in Education (McCarthy & Crichlow), 4
racial identity, 50
"radical love", 64
Rain, Steam and Speed: The Great Western Railway (Turner), 55
Rajchmann, John, 54, 57, 58, 59–60
Ravitch, Diane, 28, 30, 32, 33
Reader's Digest, 176(n3)
Reagan, Ronald, 34
recombinant DNA, 61
Redbook, 176(n3)
Reed, Ishmael, 93
"reflective practice", 178(n1)
religere, 173–174
"rememory", of Morrison, 141, 143, 144, 152
rewritten histories, 34
The Right, 30
Robinson, Douglas, 54
Roman, Leslie, 178(n2)
romance novels, 138, 142, 151
Rooney, Ellen, 24
Rugg, Harold, 3

St. Augustine, 64, 65
St. Paul, 64, 65
"schizoanalytic" theories, 72
schizophrenia, 67–68, 84
  language and literature of, 51–53